In the Long Run . . .

Longitudinal Studies of Psychopathology in Children

The GAP Committee on Child Psychiatry gratefully acknowledges the editorial assistance of Amy Willard, Division of Child and Adolescent Psychiatry, Department of Psychiatry, University of Louisville, Louisville, Kentucky, in the final editing and production of the manuscript.

Committee on Child Psychiatry

Peter E. Tanguay, M.D., *Chairperson*
James M. Bell, M.D.
H. Donald Dunton, M.D.
Joseph Fischhoff, M.D.
Peter S. Jensen, M.D.
John F. McDermott Jr., M.D.
David Mrazek, M.D.
Cynthia Pfeffer, M.D.
John E. Schowalter, M.D.
Theodore Shapiro, M.D.
Lenore Terr, M.D.
Revised by Penelope Knapp, M.D.
Anthony Poehailos, M.D. (Fellow)
Mercedes Martinez, M.D. (Fellow)

In the Long Run . . .

Longitudinal Studies of Psychopathology in Children

Formulated by the
Committee on Child Psychiatry

Group for the Advancement of Psychiatry
Report No. 143

American
Psychiatric
Press, Inc.

Washington, DC
London, England

Published by American Psychiatric Press, Inc.
1400 K Street, N.W., Washington, DC   20005
www.appi.org

Library of Congress Cataloging-in-Publication Data
In the long run—longitudinal studies of psychopathology in children /
   formulated by the Committee on Child Psychiatry, Group for the
   Advancement of Psychiatry. — 1st ed.
       p.   cm. — (Report ; no. 143)
     Includes bibliographical references and index.
     ISBN 0-87318-211-1 (alk. paper)
     1. Child psychopathology—Longitudinal studies.   2. Mentally ill
   children—Longitudinal studies.   I. Group for the Advancement of
   Psychiatry.   Committee on Child Psychiatry.   II. Series: Report
   (Group for the Advancement of Psychiatry : 1984) ; no. 143.
     [DNML: 1. Mental Disorders—in infancy & childhood.
     2. Longitudinal Studies—in infancy & childhood.   W1RE209BR no. 143
     1998]
   RC321.G7 no. 143
   [RJ499]
   618.92′89—dc21
   DNLM/DLC
   for Library of Congress   98-29255
                                                                         CIP

British Library Cataloguing in Publication Data
A CIP record is available from the British Library.

Contents

1

Introduction and Overview

Will they or won't they outgrow it? Which childhood mental health problems lead to later psychopathology? Longitudinal studies (defined as studies with a follow-up period of at least 3 years) allow the researcher to follow the developing child over time and best contribute to our understanding of these questions. The members of the Child Psychiatry Committee of the Group for Advancement of Psychiatry (GAP) undertook this review of longitudinal studies because the conclusions of many of these studies are important, but many have not been well-publicized or integrated into the child psychiatry database. Some important studies have been published as books with brief or limited circulation or in governmental reports that are hard to find. By presenting an integrated review, we hope to facilitate the work of clinicians and investigators interested in issues of primary and secondary prevention.

Some of the findings may surprise you; others may be familiar. For example, Head Start for disadvantaged children has *not* been a failure. Aggression, disruptive behavior disorders, and attention-deficit disorder in 5- and 6-year-old children, especially if they coexist with other diagnoses, may precede serious psychopathology later in development. Affective and anxiety disorders in young school-age children are associated with similar disorders in adolescence and adulthood. At least a third of adolescents with anorexia remain seriously ill in adulthood. Children whose parents are mentally ill have both a genetic and an experiential risk of developing psychopathology themselves. Although

1

temperamental traits in infancy may not persist into later childhood, temperamental traits at age 5 or 6 do persist and may predict later psychopathology.

Because we found these and other results of longitudinal studies to be relevant to everyday clinical practice, we resolved to bring them to the attention of mental health professionals, development specialists, educators, public policymakers, and parents. We selected studies that involved large populations, control groups, and proper statistical analysis and those that appeared to be generalizable. Some studies represent the efforts of many investigators; other studies are more modest.

Like all GAP reports, this report comprises chapters initially produced by only one or two individuals, but the collaborative efforts of most committee members are represented in each chapter. This review does not cover certain interesting questions. Because few studies of effects of deafness or blindness on psychological development extend to 3 years or more, we could not include a chapter on this topic. Long-term effects of divorce are clinically important, but because there have been several books already published on this topic, it is not included in this report. Several excellent longitudinal epidemiological studies, which have followed individuals from early college age to old age, tracing the influence of earlier personal and psychological attributes to later development, did not begin in childhood and therefore were not included in our report. Studies of six general syndromes are reviewed: chronic medical illness, childhood trauma, mood and anxiety disorders, eating disorders, attention-deficit/hyperactivity disorder (ADHD), and conduct disorder. We also review the long-term effects on child development of social stress, of attending Head Start, of having a mentally ill parent, and of having more than one mental disorder. We hope this volume will put into the practitioner's hand a useful reference to assist in clinical decision making.

History and Pitfalls of Longitudinal Research

Longitudinal research may teach us to better predict the outcome of a disorder and the effects of our treatment. Psychiatric diagnosis itself enables better prediction of prognosis, vulnerability, and risk than does simple symptom description. Epidemiological studies of the point prevalence of psychiatric disorders offer cross-sectional description. Studies of the incidence of psychiatric diagnosis point to information about who is most likely to fall ill, how a disorder will progress, and who is likely to survive or succumb. Such cross-sectional studies provide us with developmental information about how many and what types of children fall ill, but they do not tell us who will become ill in the general population or in a specific cohort, nor do they tell us who among the disordered will fare well or survive. Although course of illnesses has been studied with interest since the time of Hippocrates, systematic longitudinal studies are relatively recent because they are difficult to execute and require a long commitment of resources.

Epidemiological studies of childhood psychopathology are important not only to establish incidence and prevalence rates but also to increase our understanding of the causes, development, and course of childhood psychiatric disorders (Costello et al. 1993). Such studies are important not only for understanding disorders in particular children but also for learning more about the long-term effects of their disorders on other family members. For example, Faraone et al. (1996) found that 4 years after a child's initial diagnosis with ADHD, there were significant elevations of behavioral, mood, and anxiety disorders found among the child's siblings. The siblings also had high rates of school failure. This longitudinal study identifies that the siblings of children with ADHD may require primary prevention interventions, an important finding for clinicians caring for children.

Early Studies

Early studies from Berkeley and the Fels Institute (Bayley 1960) and the psychoanalytically guided studies at Yale (Kris 1957), although descriptively rich, were limited because they were essentially ahypothetical. A large corpus of data on demography, physical features, and observed adaptation was amassed. Regrettably, there was little in these studies about what data are essential to the clinician trying to decide if his or her patient will develop a particular disorder or specific personality variation.

After World War II, Margaret Fries began her studies of congenital activity type (Fries and Woolf 1953) to test the notion that the earliest activity level would be related to later drive intensity and behavior. This valiant start was the intellectual precursor to the New York Longitudinal Study

(Thomas and Chess 1982). In this study, Thomas and Chess developed nine parameters of behavior to characterize the concept of temperament. The characterization was based on animal behavioral characteristics, relatively free of traditional notions of disorder or disease. Thomas and Chess' description of the "temperamentally difficult" child was a serendipitous discovery and not a hypothesis or an intention, but it has been clinically heuristic.

More Recent Research

Longitudinal studies beginning in childhood are currently recognized as useful. To review early longitudinal studies with caution and the interest they deserve will help us design the next generation of studies with wisdom gained from the past. Issues and cautions in assessing longitudinal study results must be considered.

The first significant issue is length of follow-up. Constraints on length of investigation to 2–5 years, imposed by practical matters such as limitations on grant money and interest span of scientists, also have constrained the studies' findings. Little consideration may have been given to matters such as passing a critical boundary of age or developmental stage to secure results. Sameroff and Chandler (1975) addressed those issues directly by reviewing the long-term effects of reproductive casualty, which showed clear effects of perinatal insult 2 and 3 years after birth on cognitive and developmental measures. These effects were eclipsed by the effect of social casualty as children passed their seventh birthday. Thus, survival from ante- and perinatal insult is but one rung on the developmental ladder; interventions to improve caregiving and an environment of poverty and neglect are also shown to be needed. This review cautions us to consider that, as development proceeds, other "sleeper" effects, effects that come to light only after a period of relatively normal development, deserve study.

The preceding work points to the second issue: what measures at early developmental stages will provide predictive correlations with later behavioral or biological parameters? For example, does early postnatal activity accurately predict later drive status? If so, how would one measure the latter? Do the timing and integrative failures of early motor development in infancy that Fish (1987) described predict which children will later develop schizophrenia? How does hand-eye coordination relate to later visual motor integration? Do arousal and vigor of suck predict anything about zest for life, and how should we measure that zest in a 20-year-old? Each stage of life and development calls for its own area of measurement but, as development proceeds, we do not know what or how one measurement relates to the next or the last.

A related third issue to consider in reading longitudinal reports concerns interpretation of data. For example, suppose the earliest appearances of an attribute may suggest that 10% or 40% of a population may show a particular trait or diagnosis, and follow-up studies 3 or 10 years later show the same percentages. Unless the investigators have identified that the same individuals show the trait at both points in time, the finding may be misleading to the conclusion that the diagnosis is stable. Longitudinal study design is required to evaluate whether and to what degree the specific diagnoses or symptomatic categories persist for the individuals studied.

A fourth issue to be alert to is the variation of a single or multiple trait in a population and the relation to later pathology. Early studies of mother-infant interaction may show that children vary in their security of attachment (Farber and Egeland 1984). These categories do show good correlation in the short run from 18 months to 3 years if various adaptive functions are measured (Ainsworth et al. 1978). However, there is to date a tenuous link between insecure attachment and later pathology. Similarly, attunement in early infancy between mother and infant (Stern 1985) may vary but, if a mother-infant pair is not "well attuned," this lack of attunement may not lead to pathology or significant symptoms. We may be tempted to project our prejudices about what seems desirable as an environmental influence onto our models of pathogenesis. However, concepts of invulnerability and relative safety from untoward influence have been introduced (Anthony and Cohler 1987), and they should challenge our certainty about inevitability of the course of clinical disorders. Behavior that seems undesirable or maladaptive should not be called pathological until its context is evaluated and until the limiting factors in pathogenesis are discovered.

This point is relevant for studies of children at risk because of their presumed vulnerabilities. But even for these genetically loaded children, how can we predict the appearance of symptoms or how can we predict which at-risk children will develop them? What additional social factors are contributory? At an early age, what serves as diagnostic threshold of an adult psychiatric disorder? For example, Wender et al. (1971) show a genetic effect on adopted-away offspring of schizo-

phrenic individuals, including diagnoses in the "schizophrenic spectrum" as well as the diagnosis of schizophrenia in the grown-up
children.

Perhaps the most serious issue in reading or conducting longitudinal studies involves the creative act of developing new techniques for
study. One could devote part of a lifetime to a study that then becomes
irrelevant when a new study method is developed. Recall the long and
painstaking study of coatings of pneumococci done to generate protective serums for each specific bacterial type. In one fell swoop, penicillin
wiped out the need for this work, excellent as it was. New study techniques and their application to the behaviors of children are being developed faster than the children themselves develop. Nonetheless, we
must continue to study the emergence of psychiatric illness in the course
of childhood and continue to use the hard-won information from longitudinal studies. In that cause, this volume should provide an interpreta-
tive guide to current knowledge about facets promoting or deterring
children's development toward healthy adulthood. It may distill information gained from longitudinal study about which factors are stable in
development, which factors can be changed, and what interventions
may change them.

The book begins with a longitudinal study of prevention of
psychopathology in children—specifically, prevention through early
therapeutic school-based programs. Chapters 3 and 4 examine issues related to the effects of environmental stress and of medical issues on developing psychopathology. Chapter 5 examines the effects of mentally
ill parents on a child's development, incorporating both stress and heredity. Chapter 6 reviews the impact of trauma on development. Chapters 7 through 10 examine studies of outcome in children with specific
psychiatric diagnoses. Chapter 11 extends the work presented in Chapters 7 through 10 to consider the effect of race, gender, and comorbidity
on outcome. Progression of the chapters therefore is from more general
issues that may not have been examined in many longitudinal studies to
issues that have been examined more thoroughly.

References

Ainsworth MDS, Blehar MD, Waters E, et al: Patterns of Attachment. Hillsdale,
NJ, Erlbaum, 1978

Anthony EJ, Cohler B: The Invulnerable Child. New York, Guilford, 1987

Bayley N: Maternal behavior and personality development, in Child Development and Child Psychiatry, American Psychiatric Association Psychiatric Research Report #13. Washington, DC, American Psychiatric Association, 1960, pp 155–173

Costello EJ, Burns BJ, Angold A, et al: How can epidemiology improve mental health services for children and adolescents? J Am Acad Child Adolesc Psychiatry 32:1106–1114, 1993

Faraone SV, Biederman J, Mennin D, et al: A prospective four-year follow-up study of children at risk for ADHD: psychiatric, neuropsychological, and psychosocial outcome. J Am Acad Child Adolesc Psychiatry 35:1449–1459, 1996

Farber E, Egeland B: Infant-mother attachment: factors related to its development and changes over time. Child Dev 55:753–771, 1984

Fish B: Infant predictors of the longitudinal course of schizophrenic development. Schizophrenia Bull 13:395–409, 1987

Fries M, Woolf P: Some hypotheses on the role of congenital activity type in personality development. Psychoanal Study Child 8: 48–62, 1953

Kris M: The use of prediction in the longitudinal study. Psychoanal Study Child 12:175–189, 1957

Sameroff AJ, Chandler MJ: Reproductive risk and the continuum of caretaking casualty, in Review of Child Development Research, Vol 4. Edited by Horowitz FD, Hetherington M, Scarr-Salapatek S, et al. Chicago, University of Chicago Press, 1975

Stern D: Affect Attunement. Frontiers of Infant Psychiatry 2:3–15, 1985

Thomas A, Chess S: Temperament and follow-up to adulthood, in Temperamental Differences in Infants and Young Children: CIBA Foundation Symposium 89. London, Pittman, 1982

Wender PH, Kety SS, Rosenthal D, et al: Mental illness in the biological and adoptive families of adopted schizophrenics. Am J Psychiatry 128:302–306, 1971

2

Head Start or False Start?

Robert

Robert was 3 years old when he was enrolled in the Head Start program. He had a sister who was 18 months old. His mother was 21 years old, did not work, and had never married. There was no adult male in the household and the family's sole source of support was Aid to Families With Dependent Children. His Head Start teachers noted that Robert's speech was normal but his language was moderately delayed. Although he enjoyed playing with toys, his play was not "creative or imaginative." He did not appear to interact with the other children initially but did listen to the teachers. He was obedient but "constricted." The teacher's impressions were that he had not been exposed to many activities that were usual for a 3-year-old.

The teachers knew that the mother's financial resources were limited, and she said that raising two young children was a strain. She felt demoralized and sad, had few acquaintances, and appeared depressed to the teachers.

It was the philosophy of the program to involve the parents. They attended group meetings to discuss normal child development; parent-child interaction, including play; and community resources. Also, appropriate toys were given to the parents to encourage parent-child interaction.

Seven years later, when Robert was in the fifth grade, he was evaluated for intellectual ability, educational achievement, and social behavior. He was assessed as age-appropriate in all areas, and he did not have language delay. It had not been necessary to refer Robert to a resource room or special class for students who demonstrated academic or emotional difficulties. Robert was one of a group of Head Start children matched with a control group of children without the benefit of the Head Start program. A (statistically significant) greater number of the control group were in special classes and/or failed one or more grades at the time of assessment. The investigators concluded that the Head Start program with parents' involvement had a positive and lasting effect on Robert's academic achievement and social skills in elementary school. Incidentally, Robert's mother became self-supporting, had several friends and many acquaintances, and remained unmarried. She was not sure if she would ever marry because she appraised the marriages of a number of women she knew as a "mess." She believed that Head Start was a help to her children and herself. She expressed hope for her and her children's future.

The United States—educationally oriented, at least in spirit—was among the first nations to require compulsory elementary and secondary level schooling for all children. When, in the early 1960s, it became evident that too many children in the United States were failing in school and that many high-school graduates could not read at a sixth-grade level, there was appropriate alarm. It was noted that the children who fared the worst were predominantly from the inner cities and had parents who were poor and uneducated themselves and that many came from one-parent families. The tax structure that supports education in many states results in inner-city schools spending considerably less per pupil than suburban schools spend. Inner-city children are unlikely to attend preschool, and they may arrive at school lacking basic knowledge and skills. They may have limited vocabularies, may give one-word answers to questions, and may have never seen a children's book.

The early 1960s, the era of the War on Poverty, was a time of social hopefulness. In the tenor of the times, a decision was made to remedy the educational plight of these children. The children were failing, it was theorized, because they were not being given the learning experiences in early childhood that affluent children had. At the highest levels of government, a program was developed to reverse this inequality, a program that would give poor children a head start. The program was designed not only to help the children themselves, but also to involve their families. The program would provide not only education, but also better medical care, better nutrition, and better dental health for the children.

Head Start began in 1965 as a 6-week summer experiment and soon expanded to involve close to half a million children. Over the years, the program has expanded greatly and has been extravagantly praised by governmental leaders. In 1980, President Carter applauded it as "a program that works." In 1990, President Bush requested a $500-million increase in the Head Start budget, a 28% jump over the previous year, which would raise its total budget to more than $1.9 billion. Even more striking was Oregon Governor Neil Goldschmidt's call for an expansion of his state's Head Start program in 1990, saying that such expansion would be "the most significant—the most effective anti-drug, anti-crime, pro-education strategy" in the United States (Holden 1990, p. 1400).

But hasn't Head Start been shown to be a failure? Weren't its benefits found to be largely evanescent—completely gone by the second grade? Have people forgotten the Westinghouse study (Cicirelli 1969), which reported finding only a modest short-term increase in IQ and achievement scores for Head Start children, an effect that completely disappeared during the first two grades of elementary school? Bronfenbrenner (1964) published what came to be an especially influential report that concluded that initial gains of children participating in the program soon "washed out." Very gloomy opinions were expressed by others. On the subject of preschool enrichment, Tizard (1974) concluded

> In so far then, that the expansion of early schooling is seen as a way of avoiding later school failure or of closing the social class gap in achievement, we already know it to be doomed to failure. It would perhaps be sensible for research workers to point this out very clearly to public authorities at an early stage. This is not, of course, to say that such an expansion has no value—no one would agree that a young child should not be fed well, because his present diet will not affect his adult weight and height.

In more recent years, however, reappraisals of Head Start and other preschool programs have led to a more tempered view of its effects. These studies are not always easy to interpret, and they have not entirely silenced Head Start critics, but they deserve at least to be heard.

The Perry Preschool Project

One of the earlier studies to provide a rosier view of Head Start's success was the Perry Preschool Project of Ypsilanti, Michigan, a community near Detroit (Berrueta-Clement et al. 1984). At the time the study was begun, the community's population was racially segregated. Perry school, located in a disadvantaged neighborhood, was attended by mostly black children from low-income families. The project was initiated by black educational leaders in the community, who were concerned about the high number of high-school dropouts among black children. It was led by Eugene Beatty, the first black principal of Perry School and an educator who had already pioneered programs aimed at increasing the involvement of parents in the education of their children.

The study began in 1962 and focused on the lives of 123 youths born between 1958 and 1962. The selection of a group of 4-year-olds was designated Wave Zero and of 3-year-olds was designated Wave One. Subsequently, three additional waves were enrolled. All the children came from low-income families. Fewer than 20% of their parents had completed high school; 47% of children came from one-parent families. Children were randomly assigned to experimental and control (i.e., no preschool) groups, with each carefully matched for age, sex, IQ, parental socioeconomic status, presence or absence of father, education of mother, family welfare status, family income and size, father's employment status, and birth order. Fifty-eight children were assigned to the preschool group and 65 to the no-preschool (control) group. The curriculum in the preschools to which the experimental children were assigned was designed to improve the children's intellectual and social skills.

Children participated for 2 years, at ages 3 and 4, except for Wave Zero children, who participated for only 1 year. The school year was 7½ months long. Classes were conducted for 2½ hours each day for 5 days a week. There was one adult staff member for each five or six children. Teachers made a home visit to each mother and child for 1½ hours weekly.

Children were studied yearly between the conclusion of the program and at age 11 and again at ages 14, 15, and 19. Data were gathered by using a variety of psychometric, linguistic, achievement, and sociobehavioral instruments, as well as extended interviews with the children when they were older. Official crime and delinquency records were examined to determine if the names of the children appeared in them. Attrition was minimal, with the median rate of missing data for all measures being only 5%.

In comparison with children in the control group, children in the program were found to have received important and lasting benefits. In early childhood, they scored better on IQ tests; later, they showed improved school performance and decreased delinquent and criminal behavior. Preschool attendance improved performance by almost a factor of two on four major variables at age 19. The rates of employment and attendance at college or vocational training were nearly double for the children participating in the experimental classrooms.

The Consortium Study

Exciting as the results of the Perry Preschool Project were, they represented the experiences of a small sample of students in only one school. Even as the results were being published, other studies, most equally small, were reporting conflicting results. To remedy these conflicts, the Consortium for Longitudinal Studies was formed in 1974 to study a much larger sample of preschool intervention projects for children of low-income families; the statistical technique of meta-analysis was used in the investigation (Consortium for Longitudinal Studies 1973).

Meta-analysis is a relatively recent statistical technique to analyze a body of separate but similar experiments. The technique has generated heated controversy in some quarters, especially from those whose favorite beliefs have been belied by the results of meta-analytic studies. It resembles the more traditional and subjective "review of the literature" approach to reaching conclusions about the significance of reviewed research, except that it reaches conclusions by using quantitative mathematical techniques. This technique has been used to good effect in establishing the effectiveness or lack of effectiveness of certain interventions in the fields of cardiology and obstetrics.

The Consortium selected preschool projects that met the following criteria: 1) the study must have had a specific curriculum, 2) it must have been focused on children from low-income families, 3) the preschool part of the study must have been completed before 1969, and 4) the program must have had an original sample of more than 100 subjects. Fifteen projects were identified. All but one agreed to join in the Consortium study; among them was the Perry Preschool Project. The various studies differed in many of their details of curricula and specific interventions, but all had several points in common. They had been carefully planned and well run. Baseline data had been collected on the children, and in many instances control or comparison groups had been used for evaluation of program effectiveness. The programs had been carried out in rural and urban sites in the Northeast, Southeast, and Midwest.

The Consortium study compared data gathered at four times: 1) when subjects entered the preschool program, 2) when the preschool program was ended and subjects were ages 5–10 years, 3) when subjects were ages 10–19 years, and 4) when subjects were age 21 years. Because the Consortium study was begun when data collection was still ongoing in most of the individual projects, it was able to influence which outcome measures were collected during the later follow-up phase of many of the individual projects. This method increased the similarity of data collected in different projects.

Fourteen projects were enrolled in the Consortium study, but only eight were included in the long-term meta-analysis because the others either had data that differed too much from that collected in the other projects or the data they collected in the earlier stages were incompatible with the pooled analysis variables. Attrition rates varied for each project. By 1980, recovery rates for the original samples ranged from 31% to 100%, with a median recovery rate of 79%.

The goal of the meta-analysis was to measure differences in outcome between the program and control groups within each of the 14 projects. The significance levels (P values) found for each analysis were converted to standard scores (Z scores) and the standard scores of all projects were pooled. This approach ensured that each study had equal weight and that each program group was compared with its own control. Only the raw data collected in each project were used rather than data that had been published in ongoing project reports. For most outcome measures, analyses were done twice, once using the simplest possible technique and again using multiple regression to control for background variables such as sex of the child, mother's education, and father's presence.

The major findings of the Consortium study can be summarized as follows:

1. Well-run, cognitively oriented early education programs all increase the measured IQ scores of low-income children, and they do so to an academically important degree. The pooled results for the programs were highly significant and robust.

2. IQ scores remain statistically higher for preschool children in comparison with the IQ scores of control children for some 4 years after the end of their participation in the preschool program. These differences are not robust after the second year.

3. Achievement test scores in reading and mathematics were available from four projects. At grade three, preschool graduates performed significantly better than did control subjects on both mathematics and reading, but only the mathematics finding was robust. Differences in mathematics performance remained insignificant to grade five, but not beyond this point.

4. School competence was defined as the ability to meet the academic, social, and behavioral demands of school. Two simple measures were used to evaluate school competence: 1) was the child ever retained at grade? and 2) was the child ever placed in a special class for mentally retarded, learning disabled, or emotionally disturbed students? All eight projects had data to the seventh grade for school competence; four had data to grade 12. All projects reported a lower rate of special education placements for the preschool children at seventh grade. To summarize these results, an average of 14.5% of preschool children had been placed in special education compared with 34.9% of the control group. This difference was highly significant ($P < .001$). Similar significant differences were found between the two groups in the number of children retained for a grade.

In a related analysis, the consortium examined whether group differences in results might have been due to teacher bias. If teachers knew which children had been in preschool, they might have treated them differently from the control children. If this were the case, one would expect that the greatest differences might be seen between groups in the early school years, because in later years teachers would be much less likely to know which child was in which group. The opposite effect was found: differences in school competence between groups were smaller in the earliest grades and greatest by grades five, six, and seven. At grade 12, children in the preschool group were once more found to have significantly better school competence (as measured by grade retention and special class placement) than the control subjects.

5. Data available from four projects showed that 64.8% of preschool program children completed high school compared with 52.5% of

control children ($P < .016$ for pooled χ^2 results).

6. Three projects studied participants beyond the normal age of high-school completion. No program/control differences were found for employment rate; however, of those individuals among the experimental group who had remained in the regular classroom, more were holding jobs longer than were students who had been retained in a grade or had special classroom placement.

7. Although there were no measures of occupational aspirations and pride in achievement in the earlier stages of each project, these factors were studied at later stages of follow-up. When the preschool children were between ages 10 and 19 years, they were asked to describe something that they had done that made them feel proud of themselves. The preschool children were far more likely to respond with school or work achievements than were children from the control group ($P < .003$). In addition, when mothers of the preschool children were asked, "What kind of job would you like [your child] to have later in life?" mothers of preschool children consistently named occupations that were higher status than the occupations for which the children themselves hoped. This was not true for the mothers of children in the control group.

Summing up the results of the above analyses, consortium scientists concluded that the beneficial effects of preschool intervention were not to be found in specific measures such as IQ and school achievement scores but were demonstrated in improved attitude and school competence. Children who attended preschool, it could be argued, have increased academic confidence and better parental expectations of their success. They are less likely to be held back a grade or identified as retarded or learning disabled. Being held back a grade or placed in special education classes was highly correlated with failure to graduate from high school, which correlated with later unemployment.

As promising as the results of the Consortium study were, their shortcomings must be noted. The number of programs studied was small. Even their applicability to Head Start could be questioned, since only 2 of the 11 programs in the Consortium study were run by Head Start. This factor may not have been too important, since a more recent comparison of Head Start and non-Head Start preschool programs (Lee et al. 1990) found that both had equally good outcomes as measured in early elementary school.

Study of Head Start Programs

Few Head Start programs were designed with research or long-term follow-up in mind. The most comprehensive review of the effects of Head Start is provided by the Head Start Evaluation, Synthesis and Utilization Project (McKey et al. 1985), carried out by CSR Incorporated under contract to the Administration on Children, Youth and Families of the U.S. Department of Health and Human Services. The project examined more than 210 published and unpublished research reports from Head Start programs. Of these reports, 134 were evaluated by using traditional review methods and 76 were studied by using meta-analysis techniques. The project examined the effects of Head Start in five areas: 1) cognitive development, 2) socioemotional development, 3) child health, 4) families, and 5) communities. The findings were as follows:

1. Children's cognitive ability (as measured by psychometric and school achievement tests) showed significant immediate gain as a result of participation in Head Start. This finding, reported by most studies, was robust. Gains were greatest for children participating in Head Start programs sponsored by community action agencies and less for children in programs sponsored by public schools or multiple agencies. Highly structured academic curricula produced larger immediate gains than did traditional, cognitive, or Montessori curricula. Longer (6- to 8-hour) Head Start days correlated with markedly higher immediate cognitive gains than did shorter (2½- to 5-hour) sessions. Programs with a primary emphasis on language interaction appeared to have a higher immediate impact than programs in which language was a secondary emphasis.
2. Children in the Head Start group had significantly higher achievement scores for 2 years after preschool, but their IQ scores were higher only to the end of the first grade.
3. Head Start had an immediate positive effect on children's self-esteem, achievement, motivation, and social behavior as measured with standard instruments. The greatest difference between Head Start and control groups was in social behavior; the smallest difference was in self-esteem. Improved social behavior continued well into the third year after the end of Head Start; the gains in self-esteem and achievement motivation persisted for 1 year. Classes with a strong emphasis on language interaction were found

to have a greater effect on raising the children's achievement motivation.

4. Head Start children were considerably more likely to receive medical and dental examinations; speech, language, and developmental assessments; nutritional evaluations; and vision and hearing screening. Children in the program had a lower incidence of pediatric problems than did non-Head Start children, and they had a level of health comparable to that of more advantaged children. The Head Start children had fewer dental cavities and practiced better dental hygiene.

5. Children who attended Head Start tended to have higher calorie and essential nutrient intake than children who did not attend.

6. Despite the emphasis by Head Start on parental participation, the program has had only partial success in reaching this goal. Although many parents did participate as paid teacher aides and general assistants, parental involvement was uneven, with a core of parents contributing a disproportionate share of time. And although Head Start was shown to link families with a wide range of health and social services, it had less success in helping parents to modify their child-rearing practices, teach their children academic skills, or change their basic attitudes toward education.

7. Head Start programs have frequently begun as an integral part of a community's economic environment by providing jobs and purchasing goods and services. Head Start programs employ many minority group members, some for the first time in their adult life.

The New Haven School Development Program

Although the bulk of this chapter has examined school programs operating under the aegis of Head Start, other innovative programs also have proven themselves in the past 25 years. One such program is the New Haven School Development Program.

In 1968, representatives from the Yale University Child Study Center developed, in collaboration with the New Haven school system, the School Development Program (SDP). Schools enrolled in this model program were among the lowest-rated in the city, with poor attendance and school performance, low student achievement, and serious relationship problems among students, school staff, and parents. The program developers conceptualized many of the schools' and students' difficulties from a developmental and contextual perspective, and they focused on trying to understand the underlying problems. They employed three mechanisms to address these problems: 1) a school governance/management team, 2) a mental health/staff support team, and 3) a parents' program.

The SDP now has been implemented successfully in more than 150 schools in 14 school districts, 12 states, and the District of Columbia (Haynes and Comer 1990; Haynes et al. 1988). At least six follow-up studies of the SDP model have been conducted to date; other evaluative programs are in progress. By and large, these studies indicate significant gains in math and language learning/performance among SDP school students. In addition, these studies indicate significant increases and improvements in measures of school attendance, suspensions, classroom behavior, and attitudes toward authority. Some evidence from long-term follow-up studies suggests that the earlier difference in SDP versus non-SDP students may dissipate over time, but further studies are needed.

Head Start in the Twenty-First Century

On the basis of work done to date, we believe that good preschool preparation for disadvantaged children is one of the most promising measures available today for the prevention of later school failure. The salutary effects of preschool education on disadvantaged children are indisputable. Children enrolled in such programs show clear-cut gains in psychometric and achievement test scores by the end of the first year. Any good preschool program can be successful, but a program such as Head Start, with the weight of government behind it and with the ability to ensure long-term funding, is the best approach. Head Start not only provides the educational emphasis that other schools provide, but it also provides for better nutrition, medical and dental care, and access to other social agencies than can be provided by non-Head Start schools.

Like many public programs, Head Start always has been in danger of being taken for granted or being eclipsed by another set of priorities so that its funding would begin to melt away even as people praised its worth. Indeed, funding for publicly supported programs for impoverished families has faced serious cutbacks throughout the 1990s. Although Head Start did go through some lean years in the 1980s (Chafel 1992), more recently it has had its champions who could make a difference. During his 1988 campaign, George Bush vowed to provide "full funding" for Head Start (Rovner 1990), and on May 16, 1990, the House passed a 4-year Head Start reauthorization bill, which projected 1998 funding to be $7.7 billion for the program.

The social and economic conditions since the creation of Head Start have changed. The degree of violence found in the inner cities has escalated to the point at which it is much more difficult for parents to ensure their children's safety. Takanishi and DeLeon (1994) have urged development of linkages between early childhood and family support programs.

New York City's Project Giant Step is a specific example of improvements in Head Start. The program is supported by federal education funds and city taxes. In 1990, 6,850 children were enrolled, most of whom came from families whose annual income was less than $15,000 (Wells 1990). Each of its approximately 400 classrooms has no more than 20 students; every classroom has a teacher, a teacher's assistant, and a family aide. For every three classrooms, there is a program director and a social worker. A study of the effects of the program indicates that it had more than twice the positive impact on children's cognitive performance as other early childhood programs, including Head Start. The children also showed large gains in social and emotional development, especially in their ability to communicate and interact with adults.

Although Head Start was originally conceived by some as a brief "inoculation" against the effects of poverty and low socioeconomic status, it is clear that this concept was wrong. Head Start works and it works well, but it must be continued beyond the preschool years. A model example of how this can be done has been developed by a group from Johns Hopkins University, whose experimental program Success for All was begun in 1987 (Holden 1990). Located at the Abbottston Elementary School in Baltimore, the program serves an inner-city population of mostly black students from single-parent families who are on welfare. The program involves the entire school, although the emphasis is on grades one to three. All the teachers have received special training in remedial education and behavior management. Class size is smaller than in other inner-city schools, and each student has an individual learning plan. Tutors are immediately available to any child who begins to fall behind in his or her learning plan. Family support teams handle disciplinary problems. Health services are provided by professionals who visit weekly; there are plans to open a health clinic in the school. The program costs a premium: $1,000 more per child than in other inner-city schools. The total cost, however, is still below that spent per child in Maryland suburban schools.

In March 1994, Senator Nancy Kassebaum introduced the Head Start Quality Improvement Act, aimed at raising the quality of Head Start programs by establishing general performance measures for all grantees, strengthening training and technical assistance support, and expanding the Head-Start Transition Project, whose aim is to assist children and their families in making a successful transition from Head Start to elementary school.

For some of our students, the United States educational system has failed. This failure does not have to be. Programs such as Head Start, Project Giant Step, and Success for All provide us with solutions. Failure to implement these solutions immediately can only continue the downward spiral of education. Economically, the price we pay today for such programs will be considerably less than the price we will pay in the future if we do not act.

References

Berrueta-Clement JR, Schweinhart LJ, Barnett WSA, et al: Changed Lives: The Effects of the Perry Preschool Program on Youths Through Age 19. Monograph of the High/Scope Educational Research Foundation, No 8. Ypsilanti, MI, High/Scope Press, 1984

Bronfenbrenner U: Is early intervention effective (DHEW Publ No OHD-7424)? Washington, DC, US Department of Health, Education and Welfare, 1964

Chafel JA.: Funding Head Start: what are the issues? Am J Orthopsychiatry 62:9–21, 1992

Cicirelli VG: The impact of Head Start: an evaluation of the effects of Head Start on children's cognitive and affective development. Washington, DC, National Bureau of Standards, Institute for Applied Technology, 1969

Consortium for Longitudinal Studies: As the Twig Is Bent . . . Lasting Effects of Preschool Programs. Hillsdale, NJ, Lawrence Erlbaum Associates, 1973

Haynes NM, Comer JP: The effects of a school program on self-concept. Yale J Biol Med 63:275–283, 1990

Haynes NM, Comer JP, Hamilton-Lee M: School climate enhancement through parental involvement. Journal of School Psychology 8:291–299, 1988

Holden C: Head Start enters adulthood. Science 247:1400–1402, 1990

Kassebaum NL: Head Start. Am Psychol 49:123–126, 1994

Lee VE, Brooks-Gunn J, Schnur E, et al: Are Head Start effects sustained? A longitudinal follow-up comparison of disadvantaged children attending Head Start, no preschool, and other preschool programs. Child Dev 61:495–507, 1990

McKey RH, Condelli L, Ganson H, et al: Executive Summary: The Impact of Head Start on Children, Families and Community. Washington, DC, US Government Printing Office, 1985

Rovner J: Head Start is one program everyone wants to help. Congressional Quarterly 48:1191–1195, 1990

Takanishi R, DeLeon PH: A Head Start for the 21st century. Am Psychol 49:120–122, 1994

Tizard B: Early Childhood Education: A Review and Discussion of Research in Britain. London, Social Services Research Council, 1974

Wells AS: Preschool program in New York City is reported to surpass Head Start. New York Times, May 16, 1990, p B7

3

Effects of Early Disabilities and Social Stress on Later Development

Rockefeller and Einstein

We relish accounts of individuals who overcame developmental disability to make contributions and take significant community roles. Nelson Rockefeller, with a known reading problem, became the governor of the State of New York and a candidate for the presidency of the United States. Albert Einstein is said to have had problems learning at school and might have been identified as a child with a learning disability had the current diagnostic tools been available. His genius in mathematics and physics may have compensated for his other areas of ineptitude.

What about the modal developmentally disabled child? That child does not succeed as well as Rockefeller and Einstein did. But is there a modal developmentally disabled child? Some developmental disabilities are highly selective in the functions affected; others present more global problems. For some children with pervasive developmental disorder (PDD), the outcome for social adjustment and adaptive functioning may be poor (Venter et al. 1992). Other children with focal difficulties, such as developmental reading disorder, may adapt well and have good educational outcomes (Benasich 1993). Yet in both examples, the disorder has a significant influence on the child's learning course and may affect his or her life adaptation. In this chapter, we review conditions that may affect brain development and may produce psychopathology in children and adolescents.

Neonatal Disabilities

About 10% of babies born in the United States start life with some handicap or defect (Sameroff and Chandler 1975). These handicaps or defects range from mild learning disorders to severe mental retardation. As far back as 1947, Gesell and Amatruda introduced the notion of *minimal cerebral injury*. In 1966, Pasamanick and Knobloch articulated the concept of a *continuum of reproductive casualty*, developmental insult contributed by intrauterine anoxia, prematurity, delivery room complications, or social conditions. However, in a follow-up of the Pasamanick and Knobloch children at age 7 years, Corah et al. (1965) showed that many of the disturbances that had been present in the first 3 years of life, including IQ differences, had disappeared. This finding suggests that anoxic infants, who do poorly on testing at age 3 years or younger, may either catch up to healthy children by age 7 or may continue to lag if they are at continued risk due to low socioeconomic status (SES) or exposure to maltreatment.

Prematurity

Prematurity has been studied extensively, and prematurely born children have been shown to be at risk for later deficits in IQ. Because some studies did not adequately control for the effects of social class, Hertzig (1981) selected 66 middle- and upper-middle-class infants who had been born prematurely (weighing between 1,000 and 1,750 g) and examined them neurologically at age 8 years. Thirteen children had localizing neurological signs, whereas 20 had two or more nonfocal neurological signs. Affected children tended to be those who had sustained prenatal, perinatal, and postnatal complications. Hertzig (1981) found no significant abnormalities in IQ or in reading or arithmetic achievement scores of the children at age 8 years, but children with soft neurological signs were significantly more likely to have been in special education classes and to have had more psychiatric consultations than were the children who were free of neurological abnormality.

Cerebral Palsy

Children with severe cerebral palsy, followed up after 14 years (Klapper and Birch 1966, 1967), were found to have more psychiatric and cognitive problems as adolescents or young adults than were unaffected children. One hundred fifty-five children were examined initially, and 89 of them were located at follow-up. Of those subjects age 18 years or older, 50% had completed high school, a figure comparable to the 55% of the control population who had graduated. Normal IQ and good self-care skills were predictive of better academic performance.

Perinatal Stress

Disturbances in development as a result of perinatal stress were identified by Werner et al. (1971) in a study of 670 children in Kauai, Hawaii. Severe perinatal stress at 20 months was correlated with lower scores on infant assessment measures. However, although 34% of the entire population by age 10 years had problems, only a small proportion of these problems could be attributed to the effects of perinatal stress.

These data led Sameroff and Chandler (1975) to construct a model of a continuum of caretaker casualty, which posits that physical and medical problems account for only a small amount of the variance of later developmental outcome. Even when temperamental features are added as a predictor, social factors remain the most powerful determinant of later outcome. Sameroff and Chandler constructed a "transactional model of development," incorporating factors that must be considered in any prospective study of developmental risk factors (Seifer et al. 1992). This model has been reformulated (Rutter and Lockyer 1988; Wyman et al. 1992) to emphasize concepts of continuity and discontinuity in development.

A developmental perspective should include specific perinatal difficulties as well as risk factors or untoward events occurring at later stages in the life cycle. Protective factors, and when in childhood they may be influential, also should be variables in a model of child development (Seifer et al. 1992; Silverman 1989).

Disabilities Arising in Childhood

Malnutrition

Intrauterine insult and genetic loading may identify the baby as at risk as a newborn. But his or her developmental course will be further jeopardized by early malnutrition (Hertzig et al. 1990).

Social Stress

Rutter (1989) has investigated the effect of social factors on the development of psychopathology. The prevalence of psychiatric diagnoses in a population of children from the Isle of Wight was compared with that found in children living in an inner-London borough (Berger et al. 1975). Inner-city children showed almost double the rate of disorders. Longitudinal studies showed that symptoms of inattention and overactivity were found to be strongly associated with later conduct disturbance.

Language Delay

Cantwell and Baker (1987) studied 600 children, ages 2–16 years, referred to a speech and hearing center for a language disorder. Fifty-three percent were found to have a psychiatric diagnosis in addition to their language disorder. Of the children with a psychiatric diagnosis, 25% had attention-deficit disorder, oppositional disorder, or conduct disorder; 20% had an anxiety disorder; and 21% had mental retardation. When Cantwell and Baker (1987) restudied this population 4 years later, they found that although some children had made marked improvement in their speech, many still had learning disorders and some had newly diagnosed learning disorder in the interval. Similar findings have been reported by Beitchman et al. (1996a, 1996b), studying a group of Canadian children.

To determine the effect of conduct disturbance and learning problems on outcome, Maughan et al. (1985) studied four groups of children with and without reading delay and behavioral problems at ages 10 and 14 years. They found that, in comparison with children with good reading skills, children who had delayed reading ability in the early grades were more likely to leave school before graduating and to have poor work records as young adults. Young children who had both poor reading skills and marked behavioral problems fared the worst on follow-up. These results held even when the effect of SES was controlled for.

Mental Retardation and Pervasive Developmental Disorders

PDDs and mental retardation represent a separate and important group of diagnoses whose outcome differs considerably from the disorders discussed previously.

Follow-up of children who have been identified early in life as having severe or profound levels of mental retardation (IQ below 50) shows, as would be expected, that most remain considerably handicapped as adults. However, children with a lesser handicap (IQ scores from 60 to 75) may no longer be considered to be handicapped on follow-up. Mercer (1973) coined the phrase "the five-hour retardate" to describe individuals who appear retarded only in the academically demanding school setting, but not at home, and who later can find a place in the work force. Zigler and Balla (1977), carrying out long-term follow-up of such youngsters, found that individuals who test as mildly to moderately retarded during the school years melt into the community and live quite satisfactory lives as adults. Because of this finding, the current diagnostic system (DSM-IV; American Psychiatric Association 1994) specifies that, for a diagnosis of mental retardation to be made, both low IQ and poor social adaptation must be present. Although mild to moderately retarded persons may have good social outcome, they also may be at considerable risk for developing psychopathology (Chess 1977; Philips 1967).

The prevalence rate of PDDs is low. Autism, as defined by DSM-IV, is found in about 4–5 per 10,000 persons. If the diagnostic criteria are modified to include milder forms of the disorder, as Wing and Gould (1979) have suggested, this rate would be higher. The inclusion of Asperger's disorder in DSM-IV is a recognition that PDD is a spectrum disorder. Regrettably, DSM-IV criteria for Asperger's disorder are not based on clinical descriptions as detailed as those that led to the characterization of autistic disorder. Perhaps it was premature to designate another new diagnostic category. Rather than proliferating diagnostic subcategories, it would be clinically useful to develop a method of dimensioning the severity of the social communication problems of autism, as recommended by Shapiro and Hertzig (1991). This method might include scales to carefully evaluate the level of individual handicap in each social communication domain.

References

American Psychiatric Association: Diagnostic and Statistical Manual of Mental Disorders, 4th Edition. Washington, DC, American Psychiatric Association, 1994

Beitchman JH, Wilson B, Brownlie EB, et al: Long-term consistency in speech-language profiles, I: developmental and academic outcomes. J Am Acad Child Adolesc Psychiatry 35:804–814, 1996a

Beitchman JH, Wilson B, Brownlie EB, et al: Long-term consistency in speech-language profiles, II: behavioral, emotional and social outcomes. J Am Acad Child Adolesc Psychiatry 35:815–825, 1996b

Benasich AA, Curtiss S, Tallal P, et al: Language, learning, and behavioral disturbances in childhood: a longitudinal perspective. J Am Acad Child Adolesc Psychiatry 32:585–594, 1993

Berger M, Yule W, Rutter M: Attainment and adjustment in two geographical areas, II: the prevalence of specific reading retardation. Br J Psychiatry 126: 510–519, 1975

Cantwell DP, Baker L: Psychiatric symptomatology in language impaired children: a comparison. J Child Neurol 2:128–133, 1987

Chess S: Evolution of behavior disorder to a group of mentally retarded children. Journal of the American Academy of Child Psychiatry 16:4–18, 1977

Corah NL, Anthony EJ, Painter P, et al: Effects of perinatal anoxia after seven years. Psychological Monographs 79 (suppl 3):1–34, 1965

Gesell A, Amatruda CS: Developmental Diagnoses. New York, Paul B. Hoeber, 1947

Hertzig ME: Neurological "soft" signs in low birth weight children. Dev Med Child Neurol 23:778–791, 1981

Hertzig ME, Snow M, New E, et al: DSM-III and DSM-III-R diagnosis of autism and pervasive developmental disorder in nursery school children. J Am Acad Child Adolesc Psychiatry 29:123–126, 1990

Klapper ZS, Birch HG: The relation of childhood characteristics to outcome in young adults with cerebral palsy. Dev Med Child Neurol 4:645–656, 1966

Klapper ZS, Birch HG: A fourteen-year follow-up study of cerebral palsy: intellectual change and stability. Am J Orthopsychiatry 37:540–546, 1967

Maughan B, Gray G, Rutter M: Reading retardation and anti-social behavior: a follow-up into employment. J Child Psychol Psychiatry 26:741–758, 1985

Mercer JR: Labelling the Mentally Retarded. Berkeley, University of California Press, 1973

Pasamanick B, Knobloch H: A Developmental Questionnaire for Infants 40 Weeks of Age. Lafayette, IN, Child Development Publications, 1966

Philips I: Psychopathology and mental retardation. Am J Psychiatry 124:29–35, 1967

Rutter M: Isle of Wight revisited: twenty-five years of child psychiatric epidemiology. J Am Acad Child Adolesc Psychiatry 28:633–653, 1989

Rutter M, Lockyer A: Epidemiological approaches to developmental psychopathology. Arch Gen Psychiatry 45:486–495, 1988

Sameroff AJ, Chandler MJ: Reproductive risk and the continuum of caretaking casualty, in Review of Child Development Research, Vol 4. Edited by Horowitz FD, Hetherington M, Scarr-Salapatek S, et al. Chicago, University of Chicago, 1975

Seifer R, Sameroff AJ, Baldwin CP, et al: Child and family factors that ameliorate risk between 4 and 13 years of age. J Am Acad Child Adolesc Psychiatry 31: 893–903, 1992

Shapiro T, Hertzig ME: Social deviance in autism: a central integrative failure as a model for social non-engagement. Psychiatr Clin North Am 14:19–23, 1991

Silverman MM: Children of psychiatrically ill parents: a prevention perspective. Hospital and Community Psychiatry 40:1257–1265, 1989

Venter PA., Lord C, Schopler E: A follow-up study of high-functioning autistic children. J Child Psychol Psychiatry 33:489–507, 1992

Werner E, Bierman J, French F: The Children of Kauai. Honolulu, University of Hawaii Press, 1971

Wing L, Gould J: Severe impairments of social interaction and associated abnormalities in children: epidemiology and classification. Journal of Autism and Childhood Schizophrenia 9:11–29, 1979

Wyman PA, Cowen EL, Work WC, et al: Interviews with children who experienced major life stress: family and child attributes that predict resilient outcomes. J Am Acad Child Adolesc Psychiatry 31:904–910, 1992

Zigler E, Balla D: Personality factors in the performance of the retarded: implications for clinical assessment. Journal of the American Academy of Child Psychiatry 16:19–37, 1977

4

The Chronically Medically Ill Child

Teddy

I was sick in the night. I had a croupey cough and Papa gave me some Ipicack which had dreadful effects. Everry boddy went to Pompeii except Conie and I who stayed at home.

Theodore Roosevelt, January 5, 1870, at age 11 in Italy (Roosevelt 1928)

The published diary of Theodore Roosevelt discloses the emotional course of his grade-school years and documents the pervasive effects of his asthma upon his development. Although in most ways he was an extremely privileged and fortunate young boy, he suffered from repeated debilitating attacks of asthma throughout childhood. Through his own words, one can trace his transformation from a sickly child to one of the most outwardly vigorous and robust American leaders of the nineteenth century. Unfortunately, not all children with chronic illness are able to adapt so well.

There is an interesting history to the study of the development of children with severe chronic illness. For many years, it was considered self-evident that children with severe physical illness were likely to experience emotional pain and suffering as a consequence of their physical restrictions. However, individuals such as Teddy Roosevelt are examples of the wide variability in the outcome of these invalid children. They show that some children are apparently able to completely overcome early adversity. The pendulum of popular wisdom recently swung toward the other extreme, tilted by the force of findings that ill children suffer less than they were thought to before. These studies, focusing on cross-sectional questionnaire reports from samples of patients, find that ill children often did not endorse experiencing psychiatric symptoms. These findings have invited counterintuitive, if not misguided, declarations regarding the absence of sadness in children during the final months of terminal painful illnesses. It is ironic that stoic children who have learned to manage their feelings bravely therefore may be classified as no different from healthy peers. Subsequently, the validity of such research results has been challenged because of major methodological errors.

To explore developmental processes that allow children to cope with severe stresses, and particularly with severe chronic illness, investigations using longitudinal designs are necessary. Clues to the nature of these developmental processes may be found in retrospective reflections, but demonstrating the mechanisms by which symptoms arise requires a longitudinal effort, focusing on individual differences to define both critical risks and protective factors for emotional development.

Unfortunately, few comprehensive longitudinal studies exist and those that are available have clear limitations. However, these investigations provide the best opportunity to understand developmental processes and also have advanced the methodology to clarify etiological mechanisms.

The first of many thorny questions to be addressed in designing a longitudinal study is whether to emphasize breadth or depth. The choice of breadth or depth should depend on the investigator's central questions. Studies designed for breadth include more subjects and allow greater generalization of conclusions to a wider range of populations. Analysis of data from a large number of subjects can be done by using powerful multivariate statistical techniques to demonstrate relationships. However, the limitation of large projects is the strength of in-depth studies. It appears from recent studies that the greater the number of subjects included in a study, the more superficial has been the level of inquiry. Data on emotional processes and internal experiences of children can be collected as part of smaller intensive studies. This information is critical for better understanding the emotional development in physically ill children. The rule has been that the depth of the inquiry is inversely related to the number of subjects. At one extreme is the intensive case study, perhaps of biographical length, focusing on the success or failure of a single child, as illustrated by Teddy Roosevelt's recovery from asthma. Such stories are inspiring and can reveal some of the critical factors leading to the successful adaptation of one child, but they do not allow us to derive general principles.

The Dunedin Child Development Study

The Dunedin Child Development Study (Hood et al. 1978) is an example of how a team of investigators resolved the breadth or depth decision by recruiting a large sample (see also Chapter 7, in this volume). This study is noteworthy for a number of outstanding strengths. Key among these are 1) the large sample size, 2) the broad range of variables measured, 3) the focus on measurement of both physical illness and emotional adjustment, 4) an impressive ability to retain the study sample, and 5) the frequency of assessments over the course of the development of the children.

The sample was collected nearly 20 years ago by enrolling all children born in Queen Mary's Maternity Hospital in Dunedin, New Zealand, between April 1, 1972, and March 31, 1973. This strategy resulted in 1,139 children and families participating in the project, and the research team has been successful in maintaining a high degree of commitment to the project. The sample is well described, so it is possible to consider its degree of generalizability to other populations. In comparison with other New Zealanders (i.e., general national characteristics), the families in the study were noted to be somewhat "underrepresentative of non-Europeans and predominantly socioeconomically advantaged" (Hood et al. 1978).

Variables measured fell into four major categories. Background measures included socioeconomic status, parental education, paternal intelligence and training in child development, an assessment of the marriage, a measurement of family mobility, and a checklist of common family activities. Developmental measures included motor, language, and intelligence items. Behavioral variables were primarily limited to questionnaire data. During the early years of the study, behavioral variables were measured by "behavioral profiles," the Rutter Parent Questionnaire (Rutter et al. 1970), and child behaviors such as naughtiness, management problems, and other general difficulties. Medical indexes were a particularly important part of this study. Neurological assessments were systematically conducted, and a number of developmentally specific medical problems were monitored. These problems included enuresis, sleeping and eating difficulties, and vision and hearing difficulties. Finally, other illnesses of interest were tracked, with special attention being paid to asthma and allergy (Langley et al. 1980).

An advantage of the Dunedin study is that the progress of the research team can be followed through their consistent and regular reporting of research findings. At this point in the evolution of the study, there are about 200 reports focusing on the development of these children. Although many of the findings would have been of limited interest taken in isolation, the entire body of the work is impressive.

Intriguing Findings

Early on, the team focused on feeding, noting that more than two-thirds of the mothers in the study weaned their babies as a result of feeding difficulties and only 25% of the mothers breast-fed for more than 12 weeks (Hood et al. 1978). The investigators were surprised to find few differences in the development of children who were breast-fed longer than was customary, given the benefits that were believed to be associated with nursing (Silva et al. 1978).

Some findings were provocative. For example, no differences were found in developmental characteristics of children who had more than two childhood traumatic accidents versus those who had no accidents. This finding indicates that tracking childhood accidents as a risk factor might yield little information (Langley et al. 1980).

The study has contributed to the field by developing new instruments for initial screens of large populations. An example is a cognitive developmental screen, essentially a two-item test, that appeared to effectively identify 3-year-olds with significant difficulties (Silva 1981). A provocative finding was that family size and ordinal position seemed to have little effect on the development of children (Silva et al. 1982) but that recurrent otitis media with effusion was associated with a twofold increase in the likelihood of subsequent behavioral problems. More surprising still was a specific reported association between early bilateral otitis media and hyperactive behavior in boys (McGee et al. 1982).

Two findings exemplify the relevance of the study of emotional factors. First, a high incidence of maternal depression was noted: 8% of the mothers in the sample were identified as having major depressive disorder. This finding raised an important methodological issue. The depressed mothers' reports on the frequency of behavioral problems in their children were not confirmed by teachers' reports of the presence of such problems in these children. These conflicting reports suggested that responses of the depressed women might be biased (McGee et al. 1983). Second, relevant to long-term cognitive development, two variables—premature birth and small gestational size—were examined. Interestingly, preterm children showed normal IQ, whereas children who were small for their gestational age were shown to be at risk for lower IQ scores and greater behavioral difficulties. This finding generated the conclusion that "it is better to be born too early than too small" (Silva et al. 1984, p. 4).

This study also focused on chronic illness. There is a high incidence of asthma in New Zealand, and the disease is of considerable national interest. At age 9 years, 813 children were still participating in the study. Asthma prevalence was defined as cumulative or current; the spectrum of wheezing illness and of bronchial hyperreactivity was examined separately. Severe asthma was defined as persistent daily wheezing despite treatment. Moderate asthma was defined as recurrent wheezing occurring at least monthly and warranting regular symptomatic prophylactic treatment. Asthma was termed mild if there were at least three episodes in a year but wheezing did not occur on a monthly basis or require treatment. Asthma was classified as trivial if there were two or fewer annual episodes. By age 9 years, only two children had severe asthma, whereas 31 had moderate asthma. Eighty-one children had mild asthma in the previous year. Thirty-three children had been classified in the past as having at least mild severity. One hundred eighty-six children had experienced trivial wheezing or a current dry cough. The rest, 480 children, were completely asymptomatic for wheezing and had no known chronic illness. No socioeconomic differences between the asthmatic children and the remainder of the sample were noted.

Importantly, pulmonary function evaluations were completed for most children. Eight hundred children completed spirometric tests and 27 (3.4%) demonstrated resting air flow obstruction. Methacholine challenges in 766 asymptomatic children demonstrated findings in 176 (23%). Interestingly, 8% of children with no history of wheezing or recurrent dry cough were responsive to methacholine challenge, whereas 35% of children with previous or current wheezing did not respond to any dose of methacholine. The research team concluded that bronchial challenges by methacholine inhalation were neither sensitive enough nor specific enough to be a useful method to establish the diagnosis of asthma in epidemiological studies (Sears et al. 1986).

Summarizing the data reflecting the prevalence of asthma in New Zealand, the authors were able to conclude that 19% of the sample had experienced wheezing the previous year and 11% had wheezed in the month before assessment. In focusing on lifetime prevalence, 27.1% wheezed at least once by age 9 years. In 34 of these children, the wheezing episodes had been of sufficient frequency to require regular antiasthmatic medication (4.2%). A fascinating issue from a methodological perspective was that only 32% of all wheezing children were identified by their parents as having asthma. Those children labeled as asthmatic more often were given a bronchodilator (76%) rather than antibiotics (28%). In contrast, those children with respiratory symptoms but not identified as asthmatic received antibiotics (49%) more often than bronchodilators (28%). All but one of the children with a diagnosis of asthma received treatment.

It was concluded that asthma of mild to moderate severity was not associated with behavioral or cognitive difficulties (Silva et al. 1987). This conclusion is limited because the two severely asthmatic children were not analyzed separately but were considered only as part of a larger group of children with moderate illness, so the impact of severe asthma was not addressed.

Asthma Results Highlight Research Concerns

The strengths and weaknesses of the asthma component of the Dunedin study bring into focus several research issues. The data on prevalence and incidence of asthma are extremely valuable and provide convincing and conclusive information about the range of asthmatic symptoms in children. Additionally, the study provided improved methodologies for assessment of illness. The high false-negative and false-positive rates in approaching the diagnosis of asthma exclusively through methacholine challenge should dissuade investigators from using methacholine challenge results in isolation. Also important is the finding that, in this sample, children with mild or even moderately severe asthma had limited risk for cognitive or emotional disturbance.

Answers to other questions were less clear. Not enough data were gathered to predict the impact of severe illness. The measures of psychological adaptation, although well documented, were of limited sensitivity and would overlook symptoms that would be of particular interest related to the impact of chronic illness of even moderate severity. Important examples are 1) dimensions of self-reported affective symptoms, 2) documentation of coping strategies, and 3) measurement of dimensions of self-esteem. A final limitation of this study is that, even though it was longitudinal, the primary focus was on defining the risk factors associated with the initial development of asthma.

W. T. Grant/National Jewish Center Study

Contrasting large epidemiological samples are in-depth assessments of children at increased risk for development of a specific disorder. The W. T. Grant/National Jewish Center Study (Mrazek and Klinnert 1990) is an example of this strategy. A central question was to define risk factors hypothesized to be associated with asthma onset. Consequently, intensive data were prospectively collected to define the early parent-child relationship and the emotional adjustment of parents.

Children of asthmatic parents are at elevated risk for developing the illness. A strategy for defining a cohort of children likely to be sensitive to risk factors would be to study the offspring of asthmatic individuals. The estimated rate for asthma in families with one affected parent is 20%; the occurrence of asthma in families where both parents are affected is approximately 50%.

One hundred fifty asthmatic families were recruited into the study in the third trimester of the mother's pregnancy with the index child. All mothers were asthmatic, and 60 (40%) of the children had a first- or second-degree paternal relative with asthma. Of these 60 families, 28 of the fathers themselves were asthmatic. Given this high genetic loading, it is not surprising that by age 3 years, 21 of these children had developed asthma. Twelve more children had developed asthma by their third birthday. Initial analyses revealed that elevated levels of immunoglobulin E antibody and early emotional stressors (Mrazek and Klinnert 1990) both predicted subsequent asthma. Psychological predictors included both clinical interviews and parental self-report life inventory questionnaires, although the semistructured clinical assessments were better indicators of subsequent risk.

There are three primary limitations of the W. T. Grant/National Jewish Center Study in comparison with the Dunedin design: 1) the generalizability of the findings are somewhat more restricted, given the characterization of the sample; 2) the ability to compare a variety of variables by using multivariate analysis is limited by the sample size; and 3) the prediction to later childhood is not possible because the study was only begun in 1985 and the children are still quite young. However, the positive associations between early stressors and subsequent development of both physical illness and emotional disturbance provide evidence for the underlying mechanisms that may relate to expression of illness. Perhaps more importantly, sufficient developmental and psychological data have been collected to examine processes related to development of psychopathology quite independent of whether the child has developed asthma.

Other Longitudinal Studies of Chronic Illness

Although many studies of physically ill children have been conducted, most are limited by short follow-up. A classic example was the creative work of Gauthier, whose pioneering studies examined the developmental course of infants with relatively mild asthma. Detailed, albeit somewhat idiosyncratic, measures of early mother-child interactions were collected, and a considerable range of patterns of relating were documented (Gauthier et al. 1977). A 2-year follow-up confirmed the absence of consistent psychopathology, but no further follow-up of the physical or emotional development of the children is available (Gauthier et al. 1978).

The classic study of Monica is an interesting contrast. Voluminous data were collected on both the physical and emotional development of this child, who had congenital esophageal atresia. Monica could not be fed by mouth until age 2 years, at which time surgical correction allowed her to eat normally. She experienced a relatively stable childhood without "other major traumata" (Viederman et al. 1979). However, many years later, Monica demonstrated lasting changes indicating memory of this early experience. For example, she repeatedly placed her own (intact) newborn for feeding in the same position that she had been placed in as an infant: supine on her lap, a position optimal for tube-feeding but not for bottle- or breast-feeding. Interesting hypotheses have been derived from this study, including speculations regarding the origins of alexithymia (the inability to express feeling states).

Conflicting Results

Conflicting results may arise from studies of psychological sequelae of medical illness if measures of psychological function are not sensitive enough. An example of this problem is a study that examined the continuity of behavioral disturbance over a 5-year period (Breslau and Marshall 1985). Two hundred fifty-five children with a wide range of physical disabilities were evaluated initially when they were ages 8–16 years. After 5 years, children with cystic fibrosis did well in contrast with children who had neurological problems, whose serious psychological disturbances persisted. Although it was encouraging that children with cystic fibrosis as a group might have fewer psychological sequelae than might children with neurological deficits, the acceptance and interpretation of these results must be tempered because the exclusive methodology was a questionnaire format. In contrast, cross-sectional studies, such as the work of Steinhausen et al. (1983), demonstrated an association between severity of cystic fibrosis and emotional disturbance.

Results of separate studies may conflict for other reasons as well. Shorter-term studies, such as Herndon et al.'s (1986) investigation of children with serious burns over 80% of their total body surface, demonstrated that survivors might have serious psychological sequelae. Their problems included excessive fears and immature behavior, although many of these children also had evident strength. Longer follow-up, by questionnaire, found more encouraging results (Browne et al. 1985). Only 15% of children with severe burns had psychological sequelae after 12 years. Long-term studies are required to test the hypothesis that "time heals all wounds."

In designing a longitudinal study, the investigator must choose the most salient questions that can be addressed and devise ways to collect appropriate data. An ongoing complex study of recently diagnosed diabetic children by Kovacs explores family and maternal variables. Ninety-five diabetic children are being followed, but these children have been recruited over the course of 9 years, and follow-up thus ranges from 2 to 11 years (Kovacs et al. 1990). The investigators have focused much of their analyses on data defining maternal emotional response to the child's illness and course, but considerable potential exists for exploring the interactions between diabetes and emotional development.

Longitudinal investigators have sometimes tried to extend their range of inquiry by adding retrospective data. An example is the study of migraine by Merikangas et al. (1990). A cohort of 457 young adults was followed for approximately 8 years. Retrospective interviews also explored the onset of symptoms that occurred during adolescence. Using this reconstructive method, the investigators found that a sequence of symptoms appears common, with episodes of anxiety preceding the first migraine attacks by 1 or 2 years and depressive episodes occurring after the onset of migraine (Merikangas et al. 1990). A prospective design is necessary to verify these relationships.

The value of conducting longitudinal studies that are designed to examine the interaction between physical and emotional development has never been so obvious. Early illnesses of childhood present specific challenges to both the affected children and their families. Advances in molecular genetics make it increasingly straightforward to identify children at risk for developing a wide range of diseases. Carefully designed, well-focused studies that prospectively measure physiological and psychological risk factors offer a good possibility for developing strategies that may minimize the likelihood of disease expression.

References

Breslau N, Marshall IA: Psychological disturbance in children with physical disabilities: continuity and change in a five-year follow-up. J Abnorm Child Psychol 13:199–215, 1985

Browne G, Byrne C, Brown B, et al: Psychosocial adjustment of burn survivors. Burns, Including Thermal Injury 12:28–35, 1985

Gauthier Y, Fortin C, Drapeau P, et al: The mother-child relationship and the development of autonomy and self-assertion in young (14–30 months) asthmatic children. Journal of the American Academy of Child Psychiatry 16: 109–131, 1977

Gauthier Y, Fortin C, Drapeau P, et al: Follow-up study of 35 asthmatic preschool children. Journal of the American Academy of Child Psychiatry 17:679–694, 1978

Herndon DN, LeMaster J, Beard S, et al: The quality of life after major thermal injury in children: an analysis of 12 survivors with greater than or equal to 80% total body, 70% third-degree burns. J Trauma 26:609–619, 1986

Hood LJ, Faed JA, Silva PA, et al: Breast feeding and some reasons for electing to wean the infant: a report from the Dunedin Multidisciplinary Child Development Study. N Z Med J 88:273–276, 1978

Kovacs M, Iyengar S, Goldston D, et al: Psychological functioning among mothers of children with insulin-dependent diabetes mellitus: a longitudinal study. J Consult Clin Psychol 2:189–195, 1990

Langley J, Silva PA, Williams S: A study of the relationship of ninety background, developmental, behavioural and medical factors to childhood accidents: a report from the Dunedin Multidisciplinary Child Development Study. Australian Paediatrics Journal 16:244–247, 1980

McGee R, Silva PA, Stewart IA: Behaviour problems and otitis media with effusion: a report from the Dunedin Multidisciplinary Child Development Study. N Z Med J 95:655–657, 1982

McGee R, Williams S, Kashani JH, et al: Prevalence of self-reported depressive symptoms and associated social factors in mothers in Dunedin. Br J Psychiatry 143:473–479, 1983

Merikangas KR, Angst J, Isler H: Migraine and psychopathology. Arch Gen Psychiatry 47:849–853, 1990

Mrazek DA, Klinnert MD: The effects of family life events on asthma onset (abstract). Psychosom Med 52:229, 1990

Roosevelt T: Theodore Roosevelt's Diaries of Boyhood and Youth. New York, Charles Scribner's Sons, 1928

Rutter M, Tizard J, Whitmore K: Education, Health, and Behavior: Psychological and Medical Study of Childhood Development. London, Wiley, 1970

Sears MR, Jones DT, Holdaway MD, et al: Prevalence of bronchial reactivity to inhaled methacholine in New Zealand children. Thorax 41:283–289, 1986

Silva PA: The predictive validity of a simple two item developmental screening test for three year olds. N Z Med J 93:39–41, 1981

Silva PA, Buckfield P, Spears GF: Some maternal and child developmental characteristics associated with breast feeding: a report from the Dunedin Multidisciplinary Child Development Study. Australian Paediatrics Journal 14:265–268, 1978

Silva PA, McGee R, Williams S: Family size, ordinal position, socio-economic status and child development: a report from the Dunedin Multidisciplinary Child Development Study. N Z Med J 95:371–373, 1982

Silva PA, McGee R, Williams S: A longitudinal study of the intelligence and behavior of preterm and small for gestational age children. Journal of Developmental and Behavioral Pediatrics 5:1–5, 1984

Silva PA, Sears MR, Jones DT, et al: Some family social background, developmental, and behavioural characteristics of nine year old children with asthma. N Z Med J 100:318–320, 1987

Steinhausen H, Schindler H, Stephan H: Correlates of psychopathology in sick children: an empirical model. Journal of the American Academy of Child Psychiatry 22:559–564, 1983

Viederman M, Engel GL, Reichsman FK: Monica: a 25-year longitudinal study of the consequences of trauma in infancy. J Am Psychoanal Assoc 27:107–126, 1979

5

Children Whose Parents
Are Mentally Ill

Robby

Because Robby could not pay attention in his first-grade class, the school asked his mother to have him evaluated by his doctor. The oldest of three children, Robby was described as "hyper" since birth. He was named after his father, who as a child had been diagnosed as having minimal brain disorder. The father dropped out of school in the 10th grade and had many arrests for various misdemeanors. Because of the father's drinking, Robby's parents divorced when Robby was age 2. His mother, age 24, had a high-school education. She was unemployed, and the family was on public assistance. Seen in the pediatric clinic of the local hospital, Robby was diagnosed as having attention-deficit disorder, and he was treated with dextroamphetamine.

At age 15, Robby was seen for evaluation in the juvenile court clinic. He had a long history of truancy, had twice failed grades in school, and had been arrested for breaking and entering, for selling marijuana, and, most recently, for selling crack cocaine. Psychological testing showed a general IQ of 92, a reading disability, poor impulse control, aggressivity, and low self-esteem. He was evaluated in two interviews by a child and adolescent psychiatrist, who noted Robby's lack of remorse or concern about breaking rules or laws and who found no evidence that Robby wished to change his behavior, only that he wanted to avoid consequences. Robby received a diagnosis of a moderate to severe conduct disorder, undifferentiated type.

Whether it be by genetic inheritance or by deviant parental nurturing, the children with mentally ill parents are themselves at risk to develop psychopathology. This risk was observed long before we understood medical genetics. The Old Testament (Exod. 20:5) warns that the sins of the fathers may be visited upon the children, even to the fourth generation. Certain families seemed cursed by having an inordinate number of offspring who acted demented, depressed, or just plain mean. Members of such families were likely to be shunned, to live in poverty, and to marry one another. Yet the effects of familial mental disorder need not be all negative. Andreasen (1987) and others have shown that psychiatric disorders do not necessarily preclude creativity. This observation also was made long before medical science took notice. Samuel Johnson complained that, in addition to his genius, he had inherited a vile melancholy from his father that made him mad all his life (Boswell 1906). Sadly, the odds of untoward effects of mental disorders predominate over good effects. During the last decades of the twentieth century, there has been a concerted effort to discover risk factors and weigh the odds that parents' mental disorders will be visited on their children. In this chapter, we focus on what has been learned about this issue, recognizing that nature-nurture issues are complex and our understanding of them is incomplete.

Earls (1987), Rutter (1989), and others have summarized and discussed the many studies of associations between parents' mental illness and mental illness in their children. That such associations occur more frequently than by chance is no longer questioned. Associations, however, do not explain causality. Some studies even suggest that a person's genetic makeup may influence how he or she remembers childhood (Thapar and McGuffin 1996). Teacher-turned-comedian Sam Levenson once quipped, "Insanity is hereditary; you can get it from your children." However, raising a child who is disturbed or has a conduct disorder is no joke—it is very stressful. "Levenson's Law" is frequently broken in families, with parents' illness predating the child's, and this is the rule rather than the exception. In many cases, the offspring's illness does not even occur during childhood but is first evident in late adolescence or in adulthood.

Nurturance Risk Factors

Quinton and Rutter (1988) have reviewed the effects on children of the breakdown of parenting. Mentally ill parents are prone to be more abusive, inconsistent, and/or neglectful in their child-raising styles when compared with control groups of parents. It is likely that these parent-child interactions are risk factors for disorders in the children. As already noted, parental mental illness also raises the likelihood that children will be removed from the home. Removal of a child and placement in a foster home or in an institution are in themselves additional risk factors; this is especially true when the placements become multiple.

Rutter and Quinton (1984) and others have shown that family discord has a powerful relationship to the occurrence of psychiatric disturbance in offspring. Again, the presence of a psychiatric disorder in one or both parents increases greatly the probability that family discord will occur. Family discord is seldom focused only between parents or between parents and children; it is generally shared among all or most family members. When, as is often the case, anger and hostility are complicated by other adversities, such as poverty, separation, divorce, and educational difficulties, the negative effect is enhanced.

The final parental risk factor is the use of alcohol and other drugs. A father's alcoholism produces relatively nonspecific stressful effects and an increased probability for family discord, poverty, separation, divorce, and child abuse. Of a mother's drug use during pregnancy, more is known about alcohol than other drugs. Streissguth et al. (1989) followed a large number of infants, grouped as offspring of either relatively heavy- or relatively light-drinking mothers. Central nervous system problems in the infants were seen more if their mothers had more heavy consumption. Because the worst damage to the fetus takes place during the weeks before and just after the woman's first missed menstrual period, drinking during this time is a major public health problem. By the time the drinking mother knows she is pregnant, it already may be too late to protect the child from damage that may cause mental retardation, craniofacial malformation, and attentional and/or behavioral problems.

A period of physiological drug withdrawal is observable for an infant born to a mother addicted to opioids, but evidence of an ongoing syndrome is not as clear as it is with alcohol. There is also debate as to the amount of reproductive hazard caused by maternal cocaine use (Koren et al. 1989). However, if the same mother who abused drugs during pregnancy raises the baby, poor prenatal and general health care may be followed by inconsistent parenting and an environment of poverty, child abuse, and the vicissitudes of living surrounded by persons concerned primarily with their personal need for drugs.

Hereditary Nature of Mental Disorders

The National Institute of Mental Health has emphasized the importance of genetics in diagnosis, treatment, and prevention of mental illness. Preliminary reports in the literature have identified possible genes for schizophrenia and manic-depressive disorder. Although the genetic approach has received much publicity, little evidence exists that the disorders of most psychiatric patients (those seen in psychotherapy or in most types of outpatient care) will be found either to be mainly influenced by genetic loading or significantly better managed because of future genetic findings. Indeed, there seems to be relatively little specificity in the congruity of types of mental illness expressed first by parents and then by their children (Rutter 1989).

It is now clear, however, that psychiatric disorders are not transmitted in a simple or definitive manner (Kennedy 1996). Merikangas et al. (1989) have summarized some of the confounding issues faced when attempting to identify specific genetic modes of transmission for psychiatric disorders. These issues include the complexity of the disorders. The interrelationship, for example, between mood and conduct disorder subtypes is not known, phenomenologically or genetically. There is also frequent comorbidity in persons diagnosed with a psychiatric disorder, well over 50% in almost all studies. The meaning, genetically, of this finding is still unclear. Finally, linkage studies are in a relatively primitive form, and retractions and corrections of previous findings are occurring. This problem should decrease as we move into the twenty-first century and the genome is completely mapped and sequenced. For now, one should obtain log-of-the-odds (LOD) ratio scores of 5 or 6 and replication of findings by more than one laboratory before making claim to a gene locus finding.

As is emphasized throughout this book, and as Rutter and Giller (1983) have pointed out, there is often discontinuity between psychiatric disorders experienced in childhood and adulthood. Although offspring may as children experience the same disorder that afflicts their parents, the influence of a genetic component seems more powerful for those disorders that persist into adulthood.

Studies of intergenerational transmission of psychiatric disorders are most complete and persuasive for a relatively small number of disorders. These include mood disorders, schizophrenia, and personality disorders, especially the antisocial type. Some types of alcohol abuse also seem to demonstrate a strong familial pattern.

Specific Disorders

Mood Disorders

Studies have concentrated mainly on major depression, bipolar disorder, and the interaction between major depressive disorder in parents and their offspring's risk for panic disorder or agoraphobia. Diagnostic purity and accuracy vary between studies. Simple correlations say nothing specific about what factors might be most important in causing the children's enhanced risk. Plomin and Daniels' (1987) views of genotype-environmental correlations and the impact on children of the so-called shared and nonshared family environments are all relevant and reflect the complexity of etiological forces. Additionally, almost all comparisons between parental and offspring disorders rely on reports that beg the question of "caseness." In other words, it is not clear that those adults who taught or brought up the children would have labeled the children as disordered without the appearance of research teams armed with research protocols. There certainly is not the usual strict definition of Kendell (1988) that "predictive validity is the best criterion available to us for deciding where to draw the boundary between illness and temporary distress" (p. 375).

Angold et al. (1987) studied children from families in which at least one parent had been treated for major depression and compared these children to children of parents who had no history of any psychiatric disorder. The children were matched for age, gender, and race. This study, which is part of the ongoing studies of the Yale Depression Research Unit, demonstrated the difficulties inherent in evaluations. The offspring ranged in age from 6 to 23 years. When children did not report dysphoria, parent-child agreement was good. However, children in general reported more dysphoria and other psychiatric symptoms about themselves than were reported about them by their parents. There was not a significant difference between the reported rates of dysphoria by children of the study parents and of the control parents. Without more longitudinal data, it is not possible to prove whether child or parent reports are more useful to predict etiology or to establish a clear parent-to-child rate of risk.

Another study by the same research unit (Weissman et al. 1987) compared the children of at least one parent with major depression to the children of parents with no disorder. In this study, the diagnosis was provided by a child and adolescent psychiatrist who interviewed children and parents. Prepubertal depression was uncommon but equally frequent in males and females. After age 12 years, females became more vulnerable to major depression, although the mean age at onset was equal for males and females. For all depressed children, the symptom profiles were similar. However, the depressed children of depressed parents did tend to become ill earlier and to have a greater severity of symptoms than did the depressed children of nondepressed parents. Children of depressed parents comparatively showed an overall greater prevalence of major depression, substance abuse, poor social functioning, and school problems than did children of nondepressed parents. This research group had earlier shown (Weissman et al. 1984) that if parents with major depression also had panic disorder or agoraphobia, their children were more likely than control children to have depression plus anxiety disorders. In this study, children had a threefold greater likelihood than did control subjects for separation anxiety if the parents had panic disorder plus depression.

Richman et al.'s (1982) methodologically sophisticated longitudinal study showed that 3-year-old nonsymptomatic children of depressed mothers were at heightened risk for a disorder during the following 5 years. Although many depressed children become depressed adults, it remains unclear exactly to what degree childhood depression is interchangeable with adulthood depression.

Studies (Mitchell et al. 1989; Puig-Antich et al. 1989) also have compared the mental health status of parents and other adult relatives of depressed children and adolescents with adult relatives of control children. Findings tend to show an overall increase in mental health disorders generally, with a modest skew favoring the presence of mood disorders in the probands' relatives.

In summary, mood disorders do tend to show some parent-child loading, more with bipolar disorder than with depressive illness (Blehar et al. 1988). With depression per se, the great degree of phenotypic heterogeneity suggests a substantial environmental impact on the degree to which anxiety and other behaviors commingle with or supplant a relatively pure depressive mood.

Schizophrenia

From at least the time of the studies of Kraepelin and Eugene Bleuler in the early part of this century, it has been assumed that schizophrenia is a hereditary condition. However, modern genetic studies show that when one monozygotic twin is schizophrenic, the risk for the same disorder in the other twin is well below 50% (Kendler and Robinette 1983). The lifetime risk in the general population is 1%. Therefore, both genetic and environmental factors are obviously important.

In a Danish longitudinal study of offspring of schizophrenic and control mothers, the proband offspring at age 23 years showed 8.6% with schizophrenia and 17% with schizotypal personality disorder. The rates for the control offspring were 1% each for the two conditions (Parnas 1986). The etiological model that seems most likely is that schizophrenic and schizotypal patients share the same or similar genetic loading but that additional insults are greater for those who become schizophrenic. Significant additional risks in the Danish study included fathers who were psychiatrically disordered, institutionalization of the child, and obstetrical complications. But again, it must be kept in mind that these risks are correlational and not yet proven to be causal.

Newborns whose mothers were diagnosed with schizophrenia were followed, along with newborn control subjects, for 4 years in the Rochester Longitudinal Study (Sameroff et al. 1987). Developmental examinations were performed when the children were ages 4, 12, 30, and 48 months. Although the ages of the children were still far below the usual age for the onset of schizophrenia, their developmental status was linked more to the severity of the parents' illness and socioeconomic status than the parents' specific diagnosis. Most devastating for a child was when a multiplicity of risk factors was present.

Patients with a family history of schizophrenia are less apt than schizophrenic patients with a negative family history to display findings of central nervous system disorders. The data for this finding seem to support schizophrenia as a severe final common pathway disorder resulting from the additive effects of genetic, neurobiological, and environmental factors. Studies of children not at risk who were adopted and raised by schizophrenic parents show that the variable of upbringing alone does not increase the children's risk, compared with the risk among the general population, to become schizophrenic (Wender et al. 1974). Kringlen and Cramer (1989) compared the offspring of schizophrenic monozygotic twins to the offspring of their nonschizophrenic co-twins. The latter showed fewer schizophrenic, schizotypal, and paranoid personality disorders, presumably due to more stable home environments, but the differences were not statistically significant.

Some new evidence suggests that schizophrenia and bipolar disorders may show genetic "anticipation" (i.e., they worsen with each succeeding generation [O'Donovan et al. 1995]). This finding is yet to be confirmed.

Antisocial Personality Disorder

It has long been noted that sinful fathers tend to sire sinful sons. Males carry the diagnosis of antisocial personality disorder six to seven times more frequently than do females.

Hutchings and Mednick's 1975 report from the Danish Adoption Register Study showed that if the biological father had a criminal record, his adopted-away son had a 21% likelihood of also having a criminal record. If the biological father did not have a criminal record, it did not make much difference whether or not the adopting father had one. The figures were 11.2% and 10.4%, respectively. When both fathers (nature plus nurture) had criminal records, the risk for the son to live likewise jumped to 36.2%. In a review in 1988, Robins concluded that about one-half of the children of antisocial parents will display conduct disorder behaviors. Because about 40% of males and 25% of females who have conduct disorders will be diagnosed in adulthood as antisocial, Robins calculates the risk of a child's duplicating a parent's antisocial personality disorder at about 16%.

Every study that has examined a relationship between antisocial personality disorders and alcoholism or other drug use has found a positive correlation (Drake and Vaillant 1988). The relationship seems stronger for alcohol than for other drugs.

Bohman et al. (1987) reported on a large study of children adopted in infancy. Female and male adoptees were at greater risk for alcoholism when their biological, but not their adoptive, parents were alcoholic. The most common form was mild, clearly milieu influenced, and not associated with criminality. A second type was limited to alcoholism in sons and to somatization in daughters. A third type was again expressed in daughters as somatization, whereas sons showed alcoholism with a strong tendency toward violent criminality.

A review of studies that address the issue of biological transmission of alcoholism (Pollock et al. 1987) confirms that alcoholism does indeed run in families. The degree and specificity of the influences of biological and environmental factors are not yet well understood for the children of alcoholic individuals, who are three- to fourfold more likely than others to become alcoholic. Sons of alcoholic parents seem more likely to tolerate alcohol loading better than do control males. Males with alcoholism are more likely to father both males and females with alcoholism than are control fathers. Alcoholic mothers, on the other hand, are much more likely to have alcoholic daughters than to have alcoholic sons. Although it is clear that there is a frequent overlap between alcoholism in parents and alcoholism and externalizing disorders in offspring, the mechanisms of transmission are much less clear (von Knorring 1991).

Prevention

Developing prevention strategies is hampered by our relative ignorance about the weights of various risk factors. We do, nonetheless, know some specific and general preventive steps that will make a difference in decreasing the impact of parents' psychiatric disorders on their offspring.

The most direct intervention is to work to have expectant mothers decrease or stop their use of alcohol and other drugs. This intervention is difficult for at least two reasons. First, addictions are difficult to modify. Second, fetal damage occurs very early in pregnancy. Therefore, women who are anticipating that they will become pregnant should modify or stop their drinking. Fetal damage is so common in offspring of regularly drinking mothers that public education and rehabilitation services are warranted. Every woman who abstains or drops to mild alcohol usage before pregnancy will decrease by one the number of children likely to suffer birth defects and later behavior problems.

Most preventive efforts are more general and focus on the chronically stressful environment, or "double loading," that accompanies genetic predisposition for vulnerable offspring (Silverman 1989). Mental health workers who treat adults must be better trained to ask about their patients' children and to make sure that these children receive support and, when indicated, evaluation and treatment. Although as yet there are no good data on the impact of early treatment on the long-term outcome of psychiatric illness, it is known that the separation of children from parents and the institutionalization of children worsen their long-term prognosis. Therefore, supporting a nonill parent, if there is one, can also be helpful in protecting a child from family discord, separations, and possible child abuse.

Most studies show that, although the psychiatric disorders discussed in this chapter do run in families, for a child the risk is not only for the specific familial disorder but for a spectrum of psychopathology. Therefore, any prevention strategy must balance two sets of issues. First, most offspring will not become ill at all, the type and timing of illness are never certain, and labeling might in itself bring stress to a child. Second, environmental support, early diagnosis, and intervention might make a child more comfortable and lessen the likelihood and impact of psychopathology.

References

Andreasen NC: Creativity and mental illness: prevalence rates in writers and their first-degree relatives. Am J Psychiatry 144:1288–1292, 1987

Angold A, Weissman MM, Merikangas KR, et al: Parent and child reports of depressive symptoms in children at low and high risk of depression. J Child Psychol Psychiatry 28:901–915, 1987

Blehar MC, Weissman MM, Gershon ES, et al: Family and genetic studies of affective disorders. Arch Gen Psychiatry 45:289–292, 1988

Bohman M, Cloninger R, Sigvardsson S, et al: The genetics of alcoholism and related disorders. J Psychiatr Res 21:447–452, 1987

Boswell J: Boswell's Life of Samuel Johnson. New York, Dutton, 1906

Drake RE, Vaillant GE: Predicting alcoholism and personality disorder in a 33-year longitudinal study of children of alcoholics. British Journal of Addiction 83:799–807, 1988

Earls F: On the familial transmission of child psychiatric disorder. J Child Psychol Psychiatry 28:791–802, 1987

Hutchings B, Mednick SA: Registered criminality in the adoptive and biological parents of registered male criminal adoptees, in Genetic Research in Psychiatry. Edited by Fieve RR, Rosenthal D, Brill H. Baltimore, MD, Johns Hopkins University Press, 1975, pp 105–116

Kendell RE: What is a case? food for thought for epidemiologists. Arch Gen Psychiatry 45:374–376, 1988

Kendler KS, Robinette CD: Schizophrenia in the National Academy of Sciences: National Research Council Registry: a 16-year update. Am J Psychiatry 140:1551–1563, 1983

Kennedy JL: Schizophrenic genetics: the quest for an anchor. Am J Psychiatry 153:1513–1514, 1996.

Koren G, Shear H, Graham K, et al: Bias against the null hypothesis: the reproductive hazards of cocaine. Lancet 2:1440–1442, 1989

Kringlen E, Cramer G: Offspring of monozygotic twins discordant for schizophrenia. Arch Gen Psychiatry 46:873–877, 1989

Merikangas KR, Spence A, Kupfer DJ: Linkage studies of bipolar disorder: methodologic and analytic issues. Arch Gen Psychiatry 46:1137–1141, 1989

Mitchell J, McCauley E, Burke P, et al: Psychopathology in parents of depressed children and adolescents. J Am Acad Child Adolesc Psychiatry 28:352–357, 1989

O'Donovan MC, Guy C, Craddock N, et al: Expanded CAG repeats in schizophrenia and bipolar disorder. Nat Genet 10:379–380, 1995

Parnas J: Risk factors in the development of schizophrenia: contributions from a study of schizophrenic mothers. Dan Med Bull 33:127–133, 1986

Plomin R, Daniels D: Why are children in the same family so different from one another? Behav Brain Sci 10:1–60, 1987

Pollock VE, Schneider LS, Gabrielli WF Jr, et al: Sex of parent and offspring in the transmission of alcoholism: a meta-analysis. J Nerv Ment Dis 175:668–673, 1987

Puig-Antich J, Goetz D, Davis M, et al: A controlled family history study of prepubertal major depressive disorder. Arch Gen Psychiatry 46:406–418, 1989

Quinton D, Rutter M: Parenting Breakdown: Making and Breaking of Inter-Generational Cycles. Aldershot, Hants, England, Gower, 1988

Richman N, Stevenson J, Graham PJ: Preschool to School: A Behavioral Study. London, Academic Press, 1982

Robins LN: Epidemiology of antisocial personality, in Psychiatry, Vol 3. Edited by Michels R, Cavenar JO Jr. Philadelphia, JB Lippincott, 1988, pp 1–14

Rutter M: Psychiatric disorder in parents as a risk factor for children, in Prevention of Mental Disorders, Alcohol and Other Drug Use in Children and Adolescents. Edited by Shaffer D, Philips I, Enzer N. Washington, DC, Office for Substance Abuse Prevention, 1989, pp 157–189

Rutter M, Giller H: Juvenile Delinquency: Trends and Perspectives. Harmondsworth, Middlesex, England, Penguin, 1983

Rutter M, Quinton D: Parental psychiatric disorder: effects on children. Psychol Med 14:853–880, 1984

Sameroff AJ, Seifer R, Zax M, et al: Early indicators of developmental risk: Rochester longitudinal study. Schizophr Bull 13:383–394, 1987

Silverman MM: Children of psychiatrically ill parents: a prevention perspective. Hospital and Community Psychiatry 40:1257–1264, 1989

Streissguth AP, Sampson PD, Barr HM: Neurobehavioral dose-reponse effects of prenatal alcohol exposure in humans from infancy to adulthood. Ann N Y Acad Sci 562:145–158, 1989

Thapar A, McGuffin P: Genetic influences on life events in childhood. Psychol Med 26: 813–820, 1996

von Knorring A-L: Annotation: children of alcoholics. J Child Psychol Psychiatry 32:411–421, 1991

Wender PH, Rosenthal D, Kety SS, et al: Cross-fostering: a research strategy for clarifying the role of genetic and experiential factors in the etiology of schizophrenia. Arch Gen Psychiatry 30:121–128, 1974

Weissman MM, Leckman JF, Merikangas KR, et al: Depression and anxiety disorders in parents and children. Arch Gen Psychiatry 41:845–852, 1984

Weissman MM, Gammon GD, Merikangas JK, et al: Children of depressed parents: increased psychopathology and early onset of major depression. Arch Gen Psychiatry 44:847–853, 1987

6

Childhood Trauma

Sarah

When Sarah was 5 years old and in kindergarten, the police visited her family, inquiring about the day care program the little girl had attended from ages 15 to 18 months. Sarah's father went to police headquarters and was shown confiscated pornographic photos of Sarah as a toddler, her unique birthmark fully evident on her naked body. An adult penis jabbed the child's abdomen. The young child looked confused, scared, excited, and physically uncomfortable.

Sarah's family had had no idea anything was wrong. But in retrospect, they noted that as soon as Sarah began drawing, she drew naked adults. Breast circles, nipples, and pubic hair so characterized her art productions that nursery school teachers had asked Sarah's parents what was wrong. The family was quite modest and could not explain Sarah's predilection for nudes.

On psychiatric examination, Sarah said that she was afraid of someone pointing a "finger part" at her belly. She didn't know why, but the swords that the little native dolls point at the boat passengers at Disneyland's Jungle Ride also terrified her. She could not endure the idea of someone jabbing or poking her. She believed that she might die young "in an army or something." She had almost no memory for her days in day care as a toddler, but she did say, "I think there was grave danger at a lady Mary Beth's house." Her parents never discussed the pornography with Sarah; they were too mortified about it. Sarah had no dreams and no full episodic memories that corresponded to the confiscated photograph. She was an excellent student in her kindergarten class, both socially and intellectually.

Over the past 20 years, a new syndrome of "childhood psychic trauma" has been recognized and outlined. In the early 1890s, Freud identified childhood trauma as an important etiology for adult neurotic disorders, but he abandoned this field of study in the late 1890s, and it did not again command much interest until the 1970s. Sequelae of childhood trauma do not entirely conform to the DSM-IV (American Psychiatric Association 1994) criteria for adult posttraumatic stress disorder (PTSD), but, as currently defined, childhood PTSD does have enough in common with PTSD seen in adult life to permit long-term follow-up studies employing DSM criteria. Other long-term studies employing diagnostic criteria more specific to children of course teach us more regarding children's particular responses to trauma.

We consider five major studies that have followed youngsters for more than a year after a single event, an event of enough magnitude to have traumatically affected some of them. The first, a 4- to 5-year follow-up of the kidnapped children of Chowchilla, was controlled at the 4- to 5-year mark with a matched sample of randomly selected children. The second, the Oregon Health Sciences University study of adolescent Cambodian immigrants from the Pol Pot regime, was reported at the 3-year mark. The third is a University of California, Los Angeles, study of children from a ghetto elementary school in Los Angeles that was subjected to an after-school sniper attack that killed one child on the playground and wounded several others. The 14-month follow-up of that group was reported. The fourth study is a 26-month study of children's responses to an Australian brush fire. The fifth study, more about the psychology of distant traumatic events than about the psychiatry of traumatic disorder, is a 14-month follow-up of East and West Coast youngsters originally evaluated 5–7 weeks after the Challenger spacecraft exploded.

The Children of Chowchilla

In July 1976, 26 children were kidnapped by three masked men and held captive about 27 hours until they escaped. The kidnapping consisted of three major events: 1) three men wearing stocking masks commandeered the children's summer-school bus at gunpoint and drove them into a slough; 2) the men transferred the children into two blackened vans; and 3) after an 11-hour ride with no stops for bathrooms, food, or drink, the men then put the children into a truck trailer buried in a rock quarry, where the children stayed for about 16 hours until the two biggest boys dug them out.

The study of the children of Chowchilla was the first organized, prospective study of a group of children who had been psychically traumatized (Terr 1979). Because it was the first, the researcher could not anticipate the findings ahead of time. Therefore, no structured questions or control groups could be arranged in advance of the first round of interviews, which occurred 5–13 months after the kidnapping.

Four to 5 years after the Chowchilla kidnapping, the children were seen again several times in relatively open-ended sessions. One child described clinical experiences that became questions for all of the other children in their 4- to 5-year follow-up interviews, and eventually each child answered similar questions (Terr 1983). The interesting later experiences of the Chowchilla children were then put into question form and the questions were asked in interviews with children, matched for age and sex, living in towns 100 miles away (Terr 1983). The Chowchilla findings also were tested on a consecutively arriving, age-matched control group of psychiatric outpatients evaluated in San Francisco (Terr 1992).

The long-term findings of childhood trauma at Chowchilla led to the clinical impression that every child of the 25 (one child could not be located) remained traumatized 4–5 years after the ordeal. Fears of specific kidnapping-related items (of men, strangers, cars in trouble, strange vehicles, other kidnappers, the kidnappers, or being kidnapped again) were virtually ubiquitous. The children in the group still harbored clear, detailed memories of what had happened. Despite their common wish to suppress thoughts related to the kidnapping, all could still remember the kidnapping. Later, however, more children reported memories of misperceptions related to the kidnapping than originally had made such reports. A black kidnapper, woman kidnapper, fat kidnapper, blue van, and so forth emerged from these previously clear tales of what had happened. Because the children in the Chowchilla group chose to avoid one another 5 years after the kidnapping, child-to-child spread, except within families, was not a likely reason for these growing memories of misperception. More likely, the children's initial contact with these total strangers, who had kidnapped them wearing stocking masks, encouraged the kidnapped children to "add" extra imagined abductors, to pose wider theories, and to imagine other harmful individuals still at large. Afterthinking apparently exerted considerable mental effect 4–5 years following this traumatic event.

Some of the Chowchilla children experienced a number of personal death dreams in the 4–5 years after their kidnapping. Their dreams, in general, had become symbolically disguised, enough so that the children did not realize that they were still dreaming (as they indeed were) of the kidnapping. Posttraumatic play continued up to the 4- to 5-year mark, although many of the games had been subtly shifted from "bus driver" to "mobile Barbies" or from "kidnap tag" to "tie a person to a tree and leave him or her there."

There were a number of single-incident behavioral reenactments over the 4- to 5-year period. A boy with a BB gun shot a Japanese tourist whose car had broken down outside his family's property. Never again, he vowed, would he be rendered helpless. A girl ran away from home, taking needless chances along the Southern Pacific Railway line and in a male stranger's apartment. Multiply repeated behavioral reenactments—of frozen paralysis, helpless passivity, angry rejoinders, aggressive clownishness, or inappropriate heroism—had become incorporated into 19 children's personalities. In other words, those children who had reenacted enough to develop changes of behavior now exhibited bothersome character traits, traits pronounced enough to be noted and negatively discussed by parents or teachers. One boy, who had promised himself after the kidnapping to grow strong and to be heroic, died in a freak accident hauling beef carcasses. Why he was working in such a dangerous after-school job may be speculatively linked to the trauma from 4 years before. Traumatized children tend to court danger. Accidental and traumatic death after trauma may be rare, but it is a definite long-term outcome.

A small number of Chowchilla kidnap victims experienced bodily or physical reenactments after the kidnapping. They experienced chills, stomachaches, and urinary tract urgency, feelings that originally had been connected with the kidnapping. One child exhibited very short stature and, although a proven connection could not be made to the kidnapping, other examples both in pediatrics (Patton and Gardner 1963) and in fiction (Grasse 1971) point to a linkage between external shocks and growth failure.

Possibly the most striking finding at 4–5 years after the Chowchilla kidnapping was a sense of futurelessness in the children (Terr 1983). Twenty-three of the 25 children admitted to this lack of faith in the future in their 4- to 5-year follow-up interviews. Another child mentioned this sense of futurelessness in a national news television broadcast 5 years after the kidnapping. These children expected to die young or to go through more sudden, shocking events. They could not describe their ideas for possible career choices, nor did many of them expect to marry and/or to have children. When asked for their life philosophies, many noted changes after the kidnapping. "I live day by day," or "one day at a time," several of them said. These children did not envision a good future for the world. Several fully expected the world to run out of food or to be engulfed in nuclear war.

The comparison groups to the Chowchilla children demonstrated that one could "guess" psychic trauma in those youngsters who had repetitive dreams or death dreams, played repetitive games, harbored specific-sounding fears, and showed a diminished faith about the future—either about their own futures or the world's future (Terr 1983). Most of those children who experienced a number of these findings or an intensity of one or two findings were found to have suffered in their short lifetimes one or several untoward and terrifying events. Although they could not be fully evaluated for all signs and symptoms of childhood trauma, several traumatized children were discovered in both control groups. Eight of the 25 psychiatric evaluation control subjects (Terr 1992) and 10 of 25 randomly selected small-town control children (Terr 1983) exhibited findings indicative either of severe externally generated fright or of psychic trauma. There obviously was much more terror in the world of children than previously had been anticipated.

In summary, then, the most important long-term findings in the Chowchilla studies were bright, clear, detailed memories; specific trauma-related fears; repeated play, behaviors, dreams (including of death), and bodily responses; and an impeded sense of the future. When control groups, evaluated for these same long-term changes were found to exhibit them, it was uncovered that they had been terrified or fully traumatized children. One unexpected finding at 4–5 years following the Chowchilla kidnapping was that the kidnapped children were doing well in school.

The Oregon Studies of
Cambodian Pol Pot Survivors

Cambodian adolescents who had immigrated to the Pacific Northwest following the downfall of the Cambodian Pol Pot regime (Kinzie et al. 1986; Sack et al. 1986) were followed by a group of psychiatrists. Many of the children in this study group had witnessed the deaths of their own parents in concentration camps. Most had seen horrors not to be expected in the course of an ordinary lifetime. These young people then had endured the hardships of living as "boat people" prior to immigrating to America.

Psychological and educational tests were administered to these teenagers to assess DSM-III (American Psychiatric Association 1980) criteria for PTSD and various forms of depression as well as educational competence and progress at school.

At the time of the original study, the children's average age was 17 years. They had been in the United States an average of 2½ years. Of the 40 children who had experienced severely traumatic events, 20 met diagnostic criteria for PTSD. A high percentage had depressive symptoms. Anxiety disorders and panic attacks also were relatively common (Kinzie et al. 1986). If a child lived with a family member who had survived the Pol Pot regime, that child tended to have fewer symptoms. This entire group of children, like the kidnapped children of Chowchilla, did well in school (Sack et al. 1986).

On 3-year follow-up, diagnostic interviews were conducted in the young people's homes. Sections of the Schedule for Affective Disorders and Schizophrenia (Puig-Antich et al. 1983) and of the Diagnostic Interview Schedule (A. J. Costello et al., unpublished manuscript, 1985), with additions, were administered during these interviews. The subjects also took the Beck Depression Inventory (Beck et al. 1961) and Impact of Event Scale (Zilberg et al. 1982) on their own; the Social Adjustment Scale (Weissman et al. 1981) and Life Events Scales (Sandler and Block 1979) were given by the interviewers (Kinzie et al. 1989). Twenty-seven of the original 46 subjects participated in all aspects of the 3-year follow-up. Thirteen of these subjects had PTSD, and 11 had depression (major, 8; minor, 1; intermittent, 2). Of the 13 children who had PTSD on long-term follow-up, 8 originally had received this diagnosis. Five were newly diagnosed. Three subjects with an initial PTSD diagnosis no longer qualified. Eleven of the 27 young people had not been diagnosed with PTSD at either time of study. There was some overall decrease of depression over the 3 years from 56% to 41% of the group, but depression obviously remained significant in these people (Kinzie et al. 1989).

The Cambodian students had witnessed, between ages 8 and 12 years, terrible death, destruction of human dignity, and disfigurement or defilement of bodies. Many had lost a parent or two to death. This study confirms that PTSD will occur in a large number of children if they are exposed to terrible events. It also shows that, although a few individuals improve with time, the majority experience their symptoms steadily 3 years after the initial evaluations. PTSD symptoms stabilize and persist. Of the children (41%) who did not develop PTSD over time, most exhibited avoidant behavior. Indeed, avoidance was the most likely reason for the high attrition rate in this study.

The most important point to be learned from the Oregon/Cambodian studies is that PTSD remains a persistent disorder once it is established in childhood or adolescence. Many of the children in the follow-up study by Kinzie et al. (1989) were 10 years past their traumatic events, yet they continued to be affected. A second lesson of the Cambodian studies is that depression can affect groups exposed to terrible events, often mixing with trauma and anxiety to create a trauma-depression-anxiety syndrome or some variant. The course of PTSD waxes and wanes over time. Avoidant findings persist, even in those children who were never given a clinical diagnosis of PTSD.

The Los Angeles Sniper Study

In February 1984, a man began shooting at an inner-city elementary school playground just after school was dismissed. Some children were trapped in their classrooms; some were pinned under fire on the playground; others had already left for home; and one-quarter of the student body were on vacation. A child and a passerby adult were killed in the attack and 13 children were injured.

A representative group of the student body (159 youngsters, or 14.5%) were carefully evaluated as part of a large long-term study. A structured interview was composed, geared to pick up signs and symptoms of PTSD as outlined in DSM-III. The investigators both tabulated previous life events in the child's experience and assessed the severity of the child's posttraumatic condition (Pynoos et al. 1987). The first report indicated that children would become traumatized according to their "dose of exposure" to the event. Youngsters away from the school grounds, either because they were on vacation or had left the area, were less likely to have PTSD than youngsters who were actually there. Children who were most heavily exposed (because they were on the playground near the gunfire) showed the most intrusive symptomatology and the most numbing/avoidant findings within a month of the sniper attack (Pynoos et al. 1987).

At 14-month follow-up, 100 hundred of the 159 original children who had initially been interviewed were reinterviewed with the same structured PTSD interview format. A nine-question grief inventory worked out by the authors (Nader et al. 1990) was added at this time. On follow-up at 14 months, dose of exposure continued to predict which children were most affected with PTSD. Those children who had been on the playground at the time of the shooting suffered the most posttraumatic symptoms. If a child not on the playground during the shooting had known the child who was killed during the attack, he or she was more likely to suffer traumatic symptoms a year and two months after the attack. If children originally did not have an acute traumatic reaction, they only rarely reported a new reaction 14 months afterward ($N = 1, 1\%$). Grief symptoms were independent of the amount of exposure the children had to the gunfire, and among children less exposed to the attack, there was a rapid diminution of symptoms (Nader et al. 1990).

This study emphasizes the importance of dose of exposure to the event as a factor for developing PTSD. It also shows that children who are not as seriously exposed still can develop traumatic symptomatology if they know someone who was killed during the event. The study demonstrates that 14 months into a traumatic response, the traumatic response can be expected to hold. Few symptoms go away in an intensely exposed group; however, symptoms rapidly diminish in groups who were not as directly or as closely exposed to the traumatic event.

The Australian Bushfire Study

On February 16, 1983, a large agricultural area of Australia was burned by a massive brush fire. A total of 808 children were studied on up to three occasions in the 26 months that followed the fire. At the time of the 26-month follow-up, 365 children were studied. Because this study relied entirely on parent and teacher questionnaires, no children were interviewed or directly approached (McFarlane 1987).

The prevalence of children's posttraumatic symptoms, as reported by parents and teachers, did not decrease in the period from 8 months to 26 months after the fire. When parents were scored for their own posttraumatic symptoms, their symptomatic items closely correlated with their children's symptoms, both cross-sectionally and longitudinally. Teachers' symptoms, on the other hand, did not correlate with their students' symptoms.

Although the children in this study were not seen by the research team, the overall results showed that approximately one-third of the children in the study were still preoccupied with the bushfire 26 months after it had occurred (McFarlane 1987). Certain symptoms, such as posttraumatic play, seemed to correlate to the mothers' failure to cope with the fire and their subsequent overprotectiveness of the children.

There seemed to be no one-to-one relationship between posttraumatic phenomena in the children and psychological disorder, as measured by Rutter Questionnaires administered to parents and teachers (Rutter and Graham 1967; Rutter et al. 1970). The level of a child's classroom anxiety and behavioral problems at school 2 and 8 months after the fire strongly correlated with how intense a child's posttraumatic symptoms were 26 months after the disaster. In contrast to this finding, the intensity of posttraumatic symptoms observed by the parents at 2 and 8 months after the fire was significantly correlated to the symptoms that a child had 18 months later (26 months postdisaster) (McFarlane 1987).

Twenty-six months after the fire, posttraumatic phenomena were found to be powerfully influenced by separation from parents in the days immediately after the fire, continuing maternal preoccupation with the disaster, and changed family functioning. These influences outweighed actual exposure to the fire (dose of exposure) or losses, sustained by the family, of home and personal items. Moreover, whether at 26 months a child would continue to be preoccupied with the bushfire was also affected by whether he or she had experienced other unrelated stresses. Those children who had undergone other upsetting events appeared to be more prone to be affected by the Australian bushfire of 1983 (McFarlane 1987).

This study, one in which the methodology omits the children themselves, is difficult to compare with the other longitudinal studies reported in this chapter. Dose of exposure to the fire does not appear as important in establishing a child's symptoms as was dose of exposure to a preoccupied, symptomatic mother or brief separation from the mother. Grief over a lost home or lost mementos did not seem to be a significant influence.

In an important way, McFarlane's study gives findings contrary to Pynoos et al.'s study. The methodology is an important differentiator.

Interviewing children directly can assess their posttraumatic symptoms and signs more accurately than does interviewing the parents and/or teachers. But dose of exposure, the focus of the Pynoos study, has not yet been absolutely proven to be a modulator of PTSD in childhood. In a study by Schwarz and Kowalski (1991), the authors found that PTSD was more associated with children's emotional states recalled from the disaster (in this case the Winnetka shoot-out) than it was with the children's actual proximity to the shootings or to the child who was killed. In the post-Challenger tragedy study of children's symptoms (a distant trauma), there were no detectable differences in the symptoms of children exposed to the disaster from the Cape Canaveral viewing stands and those exposed from watching the event on television in school (Terr et al. 1996).

The Challenger Spacecraft Study

A combined University of California at San Francisco-Stanford research group set out to explore how children psychologically handled a distant disaster (the Challenger spacecraft explosion) over a 14-month period. The purpose of this study was to assess what single findings of childhood trauma or what combination of findings would affect latency-age and teenage subjects—those who saw the disaster live at Cape Canaveral; those who saw it live on television in Concord, New Hampshire; or those who heard about the shocking news before seeing any television in Porterville, California (a less emotionally involved group)—and how these findings would change over a 14-month period. One hundred fifty-three randomly selected children were interviewed by one researcher using a structured interview that tested for signs and symptoms of childhood trauma and grief. Background questions were included.

The long-term results of this study are reviewed in this discussion, although the study also gives insight into healthy children's immediate responses to distant disasters. At 14 months, the majority of children interviewed on both sides of the country retained memories of the event, memories that included recollection of the spot in which they were standing or sitting, recollection of the people there at the time, and recollection of details only they could have known (Terr et al. 1996). The groups who saw the explosion live in the Florida viewing stands or on television remembered the event better than did the group from Porterville who heard first about the disaster, but more than 60% of children in both groups exhibited extraordinary retention of this event at 14 months. At 14 months, more than 65% of children on both sides of the country could visualize the disaster, although, again, a significantly higher percentage of those who had seen it live and cared more about it continued to visualize the scene. A year and two months after the disaster, more than 45% of the children showed a profound attitudinal change about the space program or about going into space. By 14 months postdisaster, more than half the teenagers indicated they had limited some of their expectations for the world's future (Terr et al. 1996).

Latency-age children responded over the 14-month study period to the Challenger disaster somewhat differently than did the adolescents. There was considerably more drawing of space-related pictures and more responses of disaster-related fantasies in the elementary-age group than in the teen group (35% versus 8%, respectively; $P = .0001$). Latency-age children avoided talk more than did adolescents (21% versus 5%, respectively; $P = .003$) and harbored more unrealistic ideas of what had happened (29% versus 8%, respectively; $P = .002$). Latency-age children also changed their minds about going into space at a greater rate than did adolescents (50% versus 16%, respectively; $P = .0001$).

By 14 months following the Challenger disaster, adolescents on both sides of the country exhibited some problems of their own. The adolescents, as opposed to latency-age children, showed a higher rate of changed attitudes about the United States (48% versus 15%, respectively; $P = .0001$). Adolescents, in comparison with latency-age children, developed more life philosophies based upon the Challenger disaster (36% versus 1%, respectively; $P = .0001$) and more pessimistic views of the world's future (58% versus 30%, respectively; $P = .001$).

Many findings related to the traumatic impact of the Challenger disaster upon children's psychologies significantly diminished over the 14-month study period (afterknowledge about the disaster, talking about it, fantasies related to it, dreams, supernatural experiences, trauma-specific fears, "mundane" fears of being alone, clinging, and feeling that there was too much thinking about it).

However, four findings held steady, or even increased, over time. Fourteen months after the Challenger disaster, more adolescents held negative attitudes about space, space careers, the United States (24% at

5–7 weeks versus 47% at 14 months; $P = .003$), and the world's future (37% at 5–7 weeks versus 58.2% at 14 months; $P = .022$) than they previously held at 5–7 weeks after the explosion.

The Challenger study demonstrates that even when investigators examine only trauma-related symptoms and signs, not the full disorder, relatively permanent effects—at least long-term effects in children—can be found. Children's attitudes and philosophies may fester, allowing, as the Challenger study shows, more children to express negative attitudes and views of the future at 14 months than at the time of impact. This finding suggests the possibility of how entire generations become Depression affected, Nazi affected, Kennedy-assassination affected, Challenger affected, or Gulf War affected. Columnist Ellen Goodman speculated that the quick, unquestioned success of the Gulf War might create a generation of war-approving children who believe that battles can solve the most complicated human conflicts (Goodman 1991). Goodman intuitively might have fallen upon one of the more striking long-term findings of the Challenger study. Attitudinal changes appeared to gain momentum over time following external, but distant and extreme, events. The findings in the Challenger study regarding memory were also worthy of note. Distant traumatic events created clear, detailed positional and people memories of a special nature. As opposed to more mundane and even more happy remembrances, these trauma-related memories tended to last.

Discussion

The clinical information gleaned about childhood trauma from the five long-term studies reviewed in this chapter is important. Although it would have been preferable to review the symptoms of traumatized children 20 and 30 years later to examine exactly how childhood traumatic symptoms lead into the traumatic syndromes affecting adults who were abused as children, no such studies are available. The conclusion to be drawn from the studies we have reviewed is that, after terrifying events, children develop certain specific signs and symptoms that mark them as traumatized. Play; drawings; sharing a bed; attitudinal and philosophical shifts; fantasies; dreams; journal, poetry, and letter writing (in teenagers); supernatural experiences; avoidance of related talk and related afterknowledge; trauma-specific and mundane fears;

posttraumatic psychological change (handwritten)

clinging; habit acquisition (e.g., nail biting, hair sucking); behavioral and psychophysiological reenactment; and personality change are some of the more important signs and symptoms of childhood trauma. Many symptoms last for considerable periods of time. A fearful child who still visualizes or feels or smells an event, who has pessimistic world views or expectations for the future, and who creatively or through "episodes," bodily sensations, or personality changes tends to repeat an aspect of some event is likely to be either traumatically "disordered" or experiencing important posttraumatic psychological changes.

Dose of exposure, the idea that those who experience the greatest, most immediate danger have the most severe PTSDs, is not incontrovertibly proven in children. Two long-term studies (McFarlane 1987; Pynoos et al. 1987) differ in their conclusions regarding dose of exposure, although Pynoos' methodology provides better data because the children themselves were interviewed. Further long-term studies are necessary to provide further answers. Dose of exposure, of course, is an important question for treatment planning. If children in the most heavily exposed group are those best predicted to develop PTSD, then school programs, mini-marathon therapy sessions, and even radio talk shows exploring PTSD must be geared to this group. The Cambodian study offers a cross-cultural wrinkle to the complexities of childhood trauma, as somatic problems (many of them psychophysiological reenactments) are found to be more common in Asian youths than in Westerners. This finding is an important reminder that cultural patterns of emotional expression must be given recognition in our clinical descriptions. It demonstrates that PTSD and depression may coexist together for years, the two sets of symptoms often intermingled into a condition much more difficult to treat than would be either PTSD or depression alone. In situations where parents or siblings die or a person is subjected to dehumanizing brutality, the combination of depressive symptoms and posttraumatic symptoms is to be expected.

Questions about psychic numbing in children remain unresolved in reviewing the five long-term studies highlighted in this chapter. Pynoos' group finds that the worst numbing and avoidance are seen in those children most dangerously exposed to a single event. The Chowchilla study indicates, on the other hand, that psychic numbing is not ordinarily a problem following single events. Many of the Cambodian children in Kinzie's and Sack's series did exhibit psychic numbing, but this group, as opposed to all the others, were repeatedly exposed to the long-term horrors of Southeast Asia and of their escape boats.

No, it is contingent upon the situation

Terr has proposed that there are two types of childhood trauma: one brought on by single events, not usually associated with psychic numbing and extreme avoidances, and the other brought on by many or long-standing events, regularly associated with psychic numbing (Terr 1991). She sees psychic numbing as developing from an anticipatory state associated with the child's knowledge that he or she will be abused again or witness horrors again. Because Pynoos' group of children lived in an inner-city ghetto, there is a chance that their direct exposures to the playground shooting was "the straw that broke the camel's back," the most recent and most frightening of a long series of frightening events. It will take more studies to answer the question regarding psychic numbing in childhood. The implications for what happens to childhood trauma in the adult's life are quite important.

Finally, there apparently are few major, controlled, prospective long-term studies on children who are the proven victims of incest, extrafamilial sexual abuse, and/or physical abuse. Abused children have many of the signs and symptoms of childhood trauma, along with the signs and symptoms of severe personality disorder, depression, dissociative personality disorder, and/or other conditions, such as attention-deficit disorder. When these abused children grow up, they tend to populate adult psychiatric hospital units and have disorders ranging from psychosis to substance abuse. As adults, they exhibit borderline states, antisocial or narcissistic personalities, and a variety of dissociative disorders. Some formerly abused children turn out healthy. Some continue to have PTSD. How do these children end up this way? What in childhood leads to the eventual results in adulthood? Obviously, these questions are extremely important to long-term follow-up study.

psychosis: contact with reality is lost in highly distorted.

References

American Psychiatric Association: Diagnostic and Statistical Manual of Mental Disorders, 3rd Edition. Washington, DC, American Psychiatric Association, 1980

American Psychiatric Association: Diagnostic and Statistical Manual of Mental Disorders, 4th Edition. Washington, DC, American Psychiatric Association, 1994

Beck A, Ward CH, Mendelson M, et al: An inventory for measuring depression. Arch Gen Psychiatry 4:53–63, 1961

Goodman E: This war may have made it look too easy. Boston Globe, March 6, 1991

Grasse G: The Tin Drum. Translated by Manheim R. New York, Random House, 1971

Kinzie JD, Sack WH, Angell R, et al: The psychiatric effects of massive trauma on Cambodian children, I: the children. J Am Acad Child Adolesc Psychiatry 25:370–376, 1986

Kinzie JD, Sack WH, Angell R, et al: A three-year follow-up of Cambodian young people traumatized as children. J Am Acad Child Adolesc Psychiatry 28: 501–504, 1989

McFarlane AC: Post-traumatic phenomena in a longitudinal study of children following a natural disaster. J Am Acad Child Adolesc Psychiatry 26:764–769, 1987

Nader K, Pynoos R, Fairbanks L, et al: Children's PTSD reactions one year after a sniper attack at their school. Am J Psychiatry 147:1526–1530, 1990

Patton RG, Gardner LI: Growth Failure in Maternal Deprivation. Springfield, IL, Thomas Publishing, 1963

Puig-Antich J, Chambers WJ, Tabrizi M: The clinical assessment of current depressive episodes in children and adolescents: interviews with parents and children, in Affective Disorders in Childhood and Adolescence: An Update. Edited by Cantwell DP, Carlson GA. New York, Spectrum, 1983, pp 157–179

Pynoos RS, Frederick C, Nader K, et al: Life threat and posttraumatic stress in school-age children. Arch Gen Psychiatry 44:1057–1063, 1987

Rutter M, Graham P: A children's behavior questionnaire for completion by teachers: preliminary findings. J Child Psychol Psychiatry 8:1–11, 1967

Rutter M, Tizard J, Whitmore K: Education, Health, and Behavior. London, Longman, 1970

Sack WH, Angell R, Kinzie JD, et al: The psychic effects of massive trauma on Cambodian children, II. J Am Acad Child Adolesc Psychiatry 25:377–383, 1986

Sandler IN, Block M: Life stress and maladaption of children. Am J Community Psychol 1:425–440, 1979

Schwarz E, Kowalski J: Malignant memories: posttraumatic stress disorder in children and adults following a school shooting. J Am Acad Child Adolesc Psychiatry 30: 936–944, 1991

Terr LC: Children of Chowchilla: a study of psychic trauma. Psychoanal Study Child 34:547–623, 1979

Terr LC: Chowchilla revisited: the effects of psychic trauma four years after a school-bus kidnapping. Am J Psychiatry 140:1543–1550, 1983

Terr LC: Childhood traumas: an outline and overview. Am J Psychiatry 148: 10–19, 1991

Terr LC: Too Scared to Cry. New York, Harper & Row, 1992

Terr LC, Bloch DA, Michel BA, et al: Children's memories in the wake of Challenger. Am J Psychiatry 153:618–625, 1996

Weissman MN, Scholomabus D, John K: Assessment of social adjustment. Arch
    Gen Psychiatry 38:1250–1258, 1981
Zilberg NV, Weiss DS, Horowitz MJ: Impact of Event Scale: a cross validation
    study and some empirical evidence supporting a conceptual model of stress
    response syndromes. J Consult Clin Psychol 50:407–414, 1982

7

Mood and Anxiety Disorders and Suicidal Behavior in Children and Adolescents

Sam

Sam is a handsome, tall, 19-year-old college freshman who is excelling academically at a large urban university. Although he hopes to put his past troubles behind him, he experiences episodic feelings of depression and repeated suicidal thoughts. In his current college year, Sam pursues many interests, such as writing, painting, swimming, and bike riding; is active in the college theater club; and has a number of close friends. The important stress experienced during the beginning of this college year was that Sam's parents moved.

During his life, Sam experienced recurrent episodes of depression, which he relates were associated with his responses to multiple family moves and his parents' chronic excessive marital problems. Sam frequently had feelings of sadness, crying episodes, feelings of hopelessness, guilt, preoccupations with death, defiant behavior, low frustration tolerance, temper outbursts, and running-away behavior. When Sam was 9 years old, his parents enrolled him in a boarding school at the suggestion of Sam's psychiatrist, who was concerned that Sam was overwhelmed and depressed by the family tensions. He attended this school until he was 12 years old, when he requested that he live at home.

During this year, the family moved across the country and Sam felt uprooted. He did not want to move and had difficulty adjusting to his new school routine. He had trouble with his peers, felt that he was teased excessively, complained that his teachers were stupid, and could not complete school assignments because he could not concentrate. Sam developed problems sleeping, threatened to harm his mother, and planned to kill himself. He ran away from home several times, once staying away for 2 days when he wandered around town contemplating killing himself with a knife. He returned home in a distraught, disorganized state. His parents immediately took him to a child psychiatrist, who was so concerned about Sam's state that he recommended psychiatric hospitalization.

Sam was hospitalized for 3 months when he was 13 years old, receiving intensive psychotherapeutic treatment and an antidepressant. His family was involved extensively in meetings with the hospital staff. When Sam showed significant improvement, he was discharged to attend a therapeutic boarding school in relatively close proximity to his home.

Sam remained in the boarding school, an environment that protected him from the daily vicissitudes of family strife, until the beginning of his senior year in high school. At that time, he moved home, on his request. Although he envisioned that senior year would be fun, he experienced a recurrence of depressive symptoms and, precipitated by a breakup with a girlfriend, took an overdose of pills he obtained in a store. He was treated by a psychiatrist for the remainder of that school year.

Just after his high-school graduation, Sam's family moved to a distant city. Sam entered college that year and lived in the dormitory. He resumed psychiatric treatment with a new psychiatrist in hopes that this intervention would help prevent recurrent depressive and suicidal states.

Sam's story highlights the profound and chronic nature of childhood depression and its potential for recovery and relapse. Although there was no family history of psychiatric problems, especially depression or suicidal tendencies, Sam's case illustrates the association between environmental stress and childhood symptoms of depression. Suicidal preoccupations, requiring intensive psychiatric intervention, occurred at the height of Sam's depressive episodes.

Recent systematic studies with children and adolescents have yielded enlightening information about the epidemiology, clinical signs and symptoms, family correlates, and physiological components of mood and anxiety symptoms and suicidal behavior. Direct observation and clinical research with children and adolescents have identified levels of impairment and long-term consequences of these states. Depression, anxiety, and suicidal behavior frequently occur concurrently in youngsters, and in certain cases feelings of anxiety and depression are part of a constellation of symptoms that fulfill criteria for mood and anxiety disorders.

Mood Disorders

The development of DSM-III (American Psychiatric Association 1980) and DSM-III-R (American Psychiatric Association 1987), with their definitions of criteria for identifying psychiatric disorders, promoted advances in understanding childhood depression as a psychiatric disorder of children and adolescents. Empirical observation of childhood symptomatology of depression dispelled previous beliefs that children are too developmentally immature to be afflicted with depressive disorders. The types of mood disorders identified in children and adolescents, which are similar to those observed in adults, include major depressive disorder, dysthymia, bipolar disorder, and adjustment disorder with depressed mood. Table 7–1 highlights main features of these disorders.

Epidemiological studies (Andersen et al. 1987; Bird et al. 1988; Costello et al. 1988) of children and adolescents estimate that the prevalence of major depressive disorder is .4%–1.8% and the prevalence of dysthymic disorder is 11.3%. The onset of bipolar disorder is rare before adolescence. Population studies suggest that cohorts of youngsters born more recently, especially since World War II, have higher rates of depression than cohorts born in earlier times (Klerman et al. 1985).

In general, the clinical characteristics of major depressive disorders are thought to be similar in preadolescents and adolescents. One study (Ryan et al. 1987) of 95 children and 95 adolescents, ages 6–18 years, who had major depressive disorder reported that, although most symptoms of depressive disorder were similar in these groups, the preadolescents had greater depressed appearance and more somatic complaints, such as headaches or stomachaches, psychomotor agitation, separation anxiety, phobias, or hallucinations, but the depressed adolescents had more lack of pleasure or interest in activities, hopelessness, excessive sleepiness, weight change, substance abuse, and lethal suicidal behavior. Other characteristics of major depressive disorder in children and adolescents

Table 7-1. Criteria for depressive disorders in children and adolescents

Symptoms	Major depressive disorder	Dysthymic disorder	Bipolar disorder	Adjustment disorder with depression
Number needed to diagnose disorder	5	2	Alternating depression and at least 3 manic symptoms (at least 1 week)	1–2
Duration	2 weeks	1 year	Days or weeks	Up to 6 months in response to stress
Depressed or irritable mood	X	X	X	X
Loss of interest or pleasure	X		X	
Weight loss or gain	X		X	
Decreased appetite	X	X		X
Insomnia	X	X	X	
Hypersomnia	X	X	X	
Psychomotor agitation or retardation	X		X	
Fatigue or loss of energy	X	X	X	
Worthlessness or guilt	X	X	X	
Hopelessness	X	X	X	X

Decreased concentration	X	X	X
Indecisiveness	X		X
Preoccupation with death	X	X	
Elevated or irritable mood			X
Grandiosity			X
Increased talkativeness			X
Racing thoughts			X
Increased goal-directed activity			X
Excessive pleasurable activities			X

include strong family history of depressive disorders, neurophy-siological indicators such as alterations in sleep patterns, and neuro-endocrine alterations such as in growth hormone or cortisol responses (Puig-Antich 1980).

Course of Childhood Depression

Complex research methods have been applied to identify the natural course of depression in young children. Studies suggest that depression presents episodes of remission and relapse throughout childhood and adolescence, often concurrently with other psychiatric disorders, especially anxiety and conduct disorders. An important finding is that when an episode of major depressive disorder is resolved, children continue to have problems with interpersonal relationships involving family and peers (Kovacs and Goldston 1991; Puig-Antich et al. 1985a, 1985b).

There have been only a few long-term follow-up studies of depressed children. The New York Longitudinal Study (Chess et al. 1983) is a classic study of child development, in which children and their parents were evaluated at periodic intervals until the children were ages 18–27 years. Among 133 children in the study, six (4.5%) had a mood disorder: two children had a major depressive disorder, three a dysthymic disorder, and one an adjustment disorder with depressed mood. The long-term symptom profiles of either major depression or dysthymia were similar during preadolescence, adolescence, and early adulthood. Children with major depressive disorder had definite family histories of mood disorders, and the children's major depressive disorder did not appear to be precipitated by situational stress. In contrast, the children with dysthymic disorder experienced chronic stress but had no family history of depressive disorders.

One of the most comprehensive prospective studies evaluating the development of children is the Dunedin Multidisciplinary Health and Development Study conducted in New Zealand with children born between April 1, 1972, and March 31, 1973 (McGee and Williams 1988). (This study also is discussed in Chapter 4 in this volume). One hundred twenty-one children were identified as having a mood disorder, and most were reevaluated at specific follow-up times. For example, at age 9 years, 6 children had a major depressive disorder, 11 a minor depressive disorder, and 23 a history of a previous episode of a mood disorder (5 had a history of a major depressive disorder and 18 a history of a minor depressive disorder). Children with a current depressive disorder, compared with those who had a history of depression or those without a history of depression, worried more and exhibited more severe antisocial behavior.

At age 11 years, 16 children had a current episode of a mood disorder and 20 a history of a mood disorder. The currently depressed children displayed significantly more symptoms of inattention, impulsivity, hyperactivity, antisocial behavior, and anxiety compared with children who either had a history of a mood disorder or had no history of a mood disorder.

At age 13 years, 16 adolescents were depressed and 21 had a history of depression. The currently depressed adolescents had significantly more symptoms of conduct disorder, anxiety/withdrawal, and psychosis than did either the adolescents with a history of depression or nondepressed adolescents.

The main results of this study suggested that depression has a chronic course, as illustrated by the finding that children who were depressed when they were age 9 years usually reported depressive symptoms at ages 11 and 13 years. In addition, antisocial and anxiety symptoms persisted concurrently with depressive episodes. Another finding was a higher prevalence of depression among boys than girls. Perhaps, as these children are followed to an older age, the prevalence of depression in females will exceed that in males, as other studies have suggested.

The most detailed prospective study of depression in preadolescents is an ongoing investigation conducted by Kovacs et al. (1984a, 1984b). Standard research instruments have been used to interview the children and their parents at regular follow-up times. In the first year of study, interviews were conducted for each child and his or her parents every 3 months and semiannually thereafter. Table 7–2 illustrates the first published reports of this study.

Co-occurrence of other psychiatric disorders (especially anxiety or conduct disorders) was frequent among these children (Kovacs et al. 1988, 1989). For example, approximately 79% of the children with major depressive disorder also had a concurrent disorder; among the children with dysthymic disorder, 93% had a co-occurring disorder; and approximately 45% of the children with adjustment disorder with depressed mood had co-occurring disorders. Table 7–3 shows the most prevalent concurrent disorders for the three diagnostic classifications.

Table 7–2.   Depression in preadolescents

	Major depressive disorder	Dysthymic disorder	Adjustment disorder with depressed mood
Number of children	42	28	11
Age at onset	9–10 years	7 years	8–9 years
Duration of first episode	32 weeks	3 years	25 weeks

Source.   Kovacs et al. 1984a; McGee and Williams 1988.

The results agree with those of the Dunedin study (McGee and Williams 1988), highlighting the co-occurrence of depressive disorders, antisocial behavior, and anxiety disorders. In this population of depressed children, the cumulative risk of developing a conduct disorder by age 19 years was 36% (Kovacs et al. 1988). Kovacs et al. (1989) noted that those children with anxiety and depressive disorders were younger than those without anxiety disorders. Anxiety disorder appeared to predate depression in two-thirds of the cases, especially among children with major depressive disorder.

When Kovacs et al. (1984a) examined the process of recovery from depressive disorders, they observed that the time to recovery was shorter in children with a major depressive disorder or an adjustment disorder than for children with a dysthymic disorder (Table 7–4).

Gender was not a factor in the rate of recovery from any of these depressive disorders; however, early age at onset was associated with more lengthy time until recovery from major depressive or dysthymic

Table 7–3.   Most prevalent concurrent disorders

With major depressive disorder (79%)	With dysthymic disorder (93%)	With adjustment disorder with depressed mood (45%)
Dysthymic disorder	Major depressive disorder	Anxiety disorder
Anxiety disorder	Anxiety disorder	Attention-deficit disorder
Conduct disorder	Attention-deficit disorder	
	Conduct disorder	

Table 7–4.   Recovery time from depressive disorders

Major depressive disorder	Dysthymic disorder	Adjustment disorder
92% in 18 months	89% in 6 years	90% in 9 months

Source.   Kovacs et al. 1984a.

disorders but not from adjustment disorder. In this study, recovery rates were not influenced by co-occurrence of other disorders or treatment. However, other reports (Keller et al. 1988) suggest that the presence of co-occurring disorders decreases the rate of recovery from major depressive disorder.

Seventy-two percent of children with an initial episode of major depressive disorder had a recurrence of major depression within 5 years (Kovacs et al. 1984a). Co-occurrence of major depressive and dysthymic disorders increased risk of developing a recurrence of major depressive disorder. Sixty-five percent of children with dysthymic disorder had a first episode of a major depressive disorder within 5 years after the onset of dysthymic disorder. None of the children with an adjustment disorder had a major depressive disorder.

Other follow-up studies have evaluated the outcome of children and adolescents with depressive disorders when they become young adults (Garber et al. 1988; Harrington et al. 1990; Kandel and Davies 1986). The results suggest that presence of mood disorders in youth populations tends to be stable and recurrence rates for depression are high. Problems in psychosocial functioning expressed as problems with peers and spouses were evident among young adults with histories of depression at an earlier age. Youth depression was associated with a greater likelihood of psychiatric hospitalization and other nonaffective psychiatric disorders, such as substance abuse, antisocial personality disorder, and generalized anxiety disorder during the young adult years.

Bipolar Disorders

There is relatively little systematic research on the prevalence and course of bipolar disorders in children and adolescents. The disorders are rare in preadolescents and more prevalent among adolescents.

Strober and Carlson (1982) reported a 3- to 4-year prospective follow-up of 60 adolescents, ages 13–16 years, who had a major depressive disorder at the time of psychiatric hospitalization. Mania developed in

20% of these adolescents during the follow-up period. Those symptoms with the greatest power to predict bipolar outcome were precipitous onset of symptoms, psychomotor retardation, and psychotic features (Table 7–5).

Although some studies (Akiskal et al. 1983) supported these findings, others (Carlson et al. 1977) did not. An important finding was reported in another investigation (Welner et al. 1979) of psychiatrically hospitalized adolescents, suggesting that within 10 years after hospitalization 25% of 12 bipolar adolescents committed suicide. This percentage represents a high rate of suicidal mortality among adolescents with bipolar disorder.

Suicidal Behavior

From a historical perspective, suicide in 15- to 24-year-olds in the United States reached its peak rate in 1977, with an age-specific suicide rate of 13.4 per 100,000 population (Eisenberg 1984). However, youth suicide was not acknowledged to be a serious mental health problem until the early 1980s, when clusters of suicide occurred among teenagers in Texas, Chicago, and New York. These suicides alarmed the general community to such an extent that strong demands were voiced to develop suicide prevention programs and institute research to advance the understanding of youth suicidal behavior.

Table 7–5. Initial symptomatology of psychiatrically hospitalized adolescents

Bipolar outcome	Nonbipolar outcome
Shorter duration of symptom onset	More severe suicidal tendencies
Intense depressed mood	Weight gain
Self-reproach	Irritability
Bodily concerns	Self-pity
Decreased concentration	Demanding
Psychomotor retardation	Significantly higher rate of family bipolar disorder
More mood congruent delusions or hallucinations	
High rate of family affective disorders	

Source.   Strober and Carlson 1982.

In 1989, the age-specific suicide rate for 15- to 24-year-olds (National Center for Health Statistics 1992) was 13.3 per 100,000 population. This rate reflects 4,870 deaths by suicide in this age group, is almost equivalent to the rate in 1977, and exceeds the rate of 12.2 per 100,000 for all ages in 1989. In contrast, the age-specific suicide rate for children younger than age 15 years is low (.7 per 100,000). These data emphasize the scope of youth suicide as a national mental health problem. Birth cohort effects identified for suicide among 15- to 24-year-olds in the United States, Canada, and Australia (Klerman 1989) are that youngsters in this age group, especially those born after World War II—the baby boom cohort—have higher suicide rates than those born earlier. Although factors associated with such cohort effects are not specifically known, they are believed to be environmentally determined rather than related to genetic alterations.

Nonfatal suicidal tendencies that involve suicidal thinking and suicide attempts are prevalent phenomena, but relatively little information exists about the outcome of youngsters who report suicidal tendencies. In studies (Cohen-Sandler et al. 1982; Goldacre and Hawton 1985; Kuperman et al. 1988; Motto 1984; Nardini-Maillard and Ladane 1980; Otto 1972; Paerregaard 1975; Pfeffer et al. 1988, 1991; Stanley and Barter 1970) with an average follow-up of .5–15 years, the rate of suicide is low, ranging from 0% to 4.3%, although one study (Motto 1984) reported that 9% of 122 psychiatrically hospitalized male adolescent suicide attempters committed suicide within an average of 10 years after hospitalization. These adolescent suicide attempters were seriously depressed at the time of their psychiatric hospitalization. Factors present at the time of hospitalization among those who committed suicide, in contrast to those who did not, were communication of intent to attempt suicide, fear of losing one's mind, seeking help before the attempt, ambivalent or negative attitude to the treating clinician, intense tendency to sleep, psychomotor retardation, and hopelessness. Some of these symptoms were similar to those described by Strober and Carlson (1982) among adolescents with bipolar disorder. Perhaps those youngsters who committed suicide were similar to bipolar psychiatric inpatients reported by Welner et al. (1979). In addition, Kuperman et al. (1988) showed that psychiatric child and adolescent inpatients are at greater risk for suicide than youngsters in the general population.

Only a few short-term follow-up studies of suicidal preadolescents have been reported. Within an average of .5–3 years of follow-up, no suicides were reported. Pfeffer et al. (1988) reported that, in 101 preadolescents selected from the community, 11.5% of the youngsters had a history of suicidal ideation or acts and 19.4% reported suicidal ideation or acts 2 years later. Four of eight preadolescents who initially reported suicidal ideation or acts reported suicidal tendencies 2 years later. This finding suggests that, within a relatively short time, the prevalence of suicidal ideation or acts is stable among preadolescents. Factors associated with suicidal ideation or acts at the 2-year follow-up were presence of a current psychiatric disorder, symptoms of chronic depression, and history of assaultive behavior.

A longer-term follow-up study conducted by Pfeffer et al. (1991) of children selected from the community and a sample of preadolescent psychiatric inpatients is ongoing. During the course of a 6- to 8-year follow-up period of 133 subjects in this study, 20 (15%) reported at least one suicide attempt, but there were no deaths. Ten youngsters reported multiple suicide attempts during the follow-up. At least 50% of these multiple suicide attempters reported approximately 3.5 suicide attempts in the follow-up period. Presence of a mood disorder during the follow-up period most strongly predicted the occurrence of a suicide attempt in the same period; adolescents who reported a suicide attempt in the follow-up period were five times more likely to have a mood disorder than adolescents who did not report a suicide attempt. A history of suicidal ideation or a suicide attempt was an important risk factor for a future suicide attempt. Delinquency and substance abuse, as well as access to firearms, have been reported to be strong correlates of adolescent suicide (Brent et al. 1987; Fowler et al. 1986).

Anxiety Disorders

DSM-IV (American Psychiatric Association 1994) classifies three anxiety disorders specifically related to childhood: separation anxiety disorder, avoidant disorder, and overanxious disorder. Table 7–6 outlines diagnostic criteria for these disorders. Epidemiological studies (Andersen et al. 1987; Bird et al. 1988; Costello et al. 1988) report prevalence rates of 1.1%–5.9% for anxiety disorders in community samples of children and adolescents. More specifically, prevalence rates in adolescents in the general population were reported as follows: overanxious disorder, 5.9%; separation anxiety disorder, 2%; simple phobia, 3.6%; and social phobia, 1.1% (McGee et al. 1990).

Table 7–6. Criteria for anxiety disorders in children and adolescents (DSM-IV)

Symptoms	Separation anxiety disorder	Avoidant disorder	Generalized anxiety disorder
Number needed to diagnose disorder	3	2	3
Duration		6 months	6 months
Worry about harm to or loss of attachment figures	X		
Refusal to go to school	X		
Refusal to go to sleep	X		
Avoidance of being alone	X		
Nightmares about separation	X		
Physical symptoms	X		
Distress when away from home	X		
Avoidance of unfamiliar people		X	
Social involvement with familiar people		X	
Worry about future			X
Worry about past behavior			X
Worry about event leading to separation from attachment figure	X		
Worry about competence			X
Somatic complaints			X

(continued)

Table 7–6. Criteria for anxiety disorders in children and adolescents (DSM-IV) *(continued)*

Symptoms	Separation anxiety disorder	Avoidant disorder	Generalized anxiety disorder
Self-consciousness			X
Need for reassurance			X
Inability to relax			X
Restlessness			X
Problems concentrating			X
Irritability			X
Muscle tension			X
Problems sleeping			X

Empirical studies suggest that anxiety disorders often co-occur with mood disorders (Costello et al. 1988) but that children with anxiety disorders are significantly younger than those with concurrent anxiety and depression (Hershberg et al. 1982; Kolvin et al. 1984; Strauss et al. 1988). Children with anxiety and depression appear to feel more anxious than those with anxiety disorder alone. Anxiety disorder also co-occurs with conduct disorder; children with these disorders are more socially impaired than children with anxiety disorder alone (Walker et al. 1991).

Important issues that require study are the characterization of symptomatology of anxiety disorders during different stages of the life cycle and the outcome of children with anxiety disorders. It is not clear whether anxiety disorders of adults, such as panic disorder with or without agoraphobia, agoraphobia without a history of panic disorder, social phobia, simple phobia, obsessive-compulsive disorder, and generalized anxiety disorder, are associated with childhood anxiety disorders. Yet these states have been reported in children—notably, panic disorder (Hayward et al. 1989; Moreau et al. 1989). Because a history of panic disorder has been associated with suicidal ideation and suicide attempts in adults (Weissman et al. 1989), the evaluation of suicidal tendencies is important in the prospective course of children and adolescents with symptoms of panic disorders.

A relation between childhood and adult anxiety disorders has been suggested: 246 girls who reported fears of thunder, animals, or injections reported similar fears as adults (Abe 1972). Thirty-three percent of these girls showed anxiety as adults. Several studies (Deltito et al. 1986; D. F. Klein et al. 1983; Pergi et al. 1988) show that agoraphobic adults reported childhood histories of school refusal, but other reports (I. Berg et al. 1976) suggest that school phobia predicts agoraphobia in only a small portion of cases. The largest study of a community sample of adults, the Epidemiological Catchment Area Study (Christie et al. 1988), conducted in five communities, suggests that a high number of anxiety disorders in adults begin in adolescence.

Course of Anxiety Disorders

The course of anxiety in childhood has received some research attention. Among nonclinical samples of children (Emde and Schmidt 1978; Gittelman 1986; R. G. Klein and Last 1989; Richman et al. 1982; Rutter et al. 1981), fears in preschool children and young preadolescents were noted to be stable during follow-up studies; such symptoms may predict other anxiety symptoms during follow-up periods. Children with fears, however, did not appear to develop conduct problems during follow-up. Research (Werry 1991) suggests that children with overanxious disorder are less likely to experience these symptoms within several years of follow-up.

Most follow-up studies focused on school refusal with underpinnings of separation anxiety or social phobia. Some studies (Baker and Wills 1979; I. Berg and Jacobson 1985; Coolidge et al. 1964; Waldron 1976; Weiss and Burke 1970) suggest that the best predictor of outcome was the clinical condition at the time of discharge from treatment. Clinical course appeared to be variable in that some children had persistent symptoms and others functioned well (I. Berg et al. 1976).

The complexities of the course of anxiety disorders are highlighted by variations in outcome associated with age at onset of anxiety. For example, school phobia with onset in adolescence may be associated with a poorer prognosis than onset of anxiety in childhood (Rodriguez et al. 1959). Among children ages 7–12 years who were psychiatrically hospitalized following school refusal (Flakierska et al. 1988), a high rate of anxiety symptoms was noted at the time of follow-up 15–20 years later. These patients, compared with those without a history of school refusal, were treated in psychiatric outpatient facilities more often as adults. In general, the few existing follow-up studies of children with school refusal suggest that there is a relatively good prognosis and less likelihood of agoraphobia in adulthood.

The most systematic research on outcome of anxiety disorders has been conducted by Rapoport and colleagues (C. Z. Berg et al. 1989; Swedo and Rapoport 1989) for obsessive-compulsive disorder. These studies suggest that the course of obsessive-compulsive disorder fluctuates with variations in severity and multiplicity of obsessions or compulsions. Chronicity of disorder is directly associated with the level of initial severity. For example, in a 2- to 7-year follow-up (C. Z. Berg et al. 1989), approximately 70% of children and adolescents originally evaluated had the disorder at follow-up. Those children with more severe disorders had higher rates of disorder at follow-up. These findings were corroborated by Hollingsworth et al. (1980). Children with obsessive-compulsive disorder exhibited problems with peer relationships and social interactions. Medication such as clomipramine is effective in reducing symptoms of this disorder (Leonard et al. 1989).

Conclusions

Because research on the course of mood and anxiety disorders and suicidal behavior is relatively scant, definitive conclusions about the outcome of children and adolescents with these problems cannot be drawn at present. Nevertheless, some findings are evident.

Children with depressive disorders are at risk for recurrent mood disorders and problematic psychosocial adjustment. The type of mood disorder is predictive of subsequent episodes of mood disorder. Children with early-onset major depressive disorder and dysthymic disorder are at risk for subsequent major depressive disorder or bipolar disorder. Children with major depressive disorder characterized by precipitous onset of symptoms, psychomotor retardation, and psychotic features may be at greater risk for developing bipolar disorder. Adolescents with a bipolar disorder are at risk for suicide.

Youth suicide and nonfatal suicidal behavior are major mental health problems. A history of suicidal ideation or attempts predicts future suicidal behavior. Youngsters at risk for suicidal behavior usually have a psychiatric disorder such as mood, conduct, and/or substance abuse disorders. Children or adolescents with such psychopathology warrant close follow-up and intervention to decrease the intensity of risk factors.

As a national mental health problem, youth suicide warrants public health efforts for its prevention. Although numerous programs have been instituted in schools to educate teenagers about risk for youth suicide, the beneficial effects of such programs are questionable (Shaffer et al. 1991). Nevertheless, prevention of youth suicide requires a multimodal effort involving community services to youth and families, public education, constraints on media descriptions of youth suicide, and increased research efforts (Alcohol, Drug Abuse, and Mental Health Administration 1989).

Minimal research exists on the course of anxiety disorders in children and adolescents. The few available studies suggest that variable outcomes can be expected and are determined by the type of initial anxiety disorder and its severity. The clearest evidence of stability of anxiety disorders is with obsessive-compulsive disorder. However, controversy exists about the continuity of childhood anxiety disorders, such as separation anxiety or social phobia, with anxiety disorders of adulthood. In general, children with anxiety disorders appear to have relatively good prognoses.

Because controlled treatment studies of the problems discussed in this chapter are rare, it is not possible to conclude whether intervention attenuates the longitudinal outcome of these problems. The most important issue to consider at the present time is that early identification of these problems and appropriate psychiatric treatment and follow-up may be helpful in limiting the morbidity and mortality associated with these psychopathologies.

References

Abe K: Phobias and nervous symptoms in childhood and maturity: persistence and associations. Br J Psychiatry 120:275–283, 1972

Akiskal HS, Walker P, Puzanfian V, et al: Bipolar outcome in the course of depressive illness: phenomenologic, familial and pharmacologic predictors. J Affect Disord 5:115–128, 1983

Alcohol, Drug Abuse, and Mental Health Administration: Report of the Secretary's Task Force on Youth Suicide (DHHS Publ No ADM-89-1621). Washington, DC, U.S. Government Printing Office, 1989

American Psychiatric Association: Diagnostic and Statistical Manual of Mental Disorders, 3rd Edition. Washington, DC, American Psychiatric Association, 1980

American Psychiatric Association: Diagnostic and Statistical Manual of Mental Disorders, 3rd Edition, Revised. Washington, DC, American Psychiatric Association, 1987

American Psychiatric Association: Diagnostic and Statistical Manual of Mental Disorders, 4th Edition. Washington, DC, American Psychiatric Association, 1994

Andersen JC, Williams S, McGee R, et al: DSM-III disorders in preadolescent children: prevalence in a large sample from the general population. Arch Gen Psychiatry 44:69–76, 1987

Baker H, Wills U: School phobic children at work. Br J Psychiatry 135:561–564, 1979

Berg CZ, Rapoport JL, Whitaker A, et al: Childhood obsessive compulsive disorder: a two-year prospective follow-up of a community sample. J Am Acad Child Adolesc Psychiatry 28:528–533, 1989

Berg I, Jacobson A: Teenage school refusers grow up: a follow-up study of 168 subjects, ten years on average after in-patient treatment. Br J Psychiatry 147:366–370, 1985

Berg I, Butler A, Hall G: The outcome of adolescent school phobia. Br J Psychiatry 128:80–85, 1976

Bird HR, Canino G, Rubio-Stipec M, et al: Estimates of the prevalence of childhood maladjustment in a community survey in Puerto Rico: the use of combined measures. Arch Gen Psychiatry 45:1120–1126, 1988

Brent DA, Perper JA, Allman CJ: Alcohol, firearms, and suicide among youth: temporal trends in Allegheny County, Pennsylvania, 1960 to 1983. JAMA 257:3369–3372, 1987

Carlson GA, Davenport YB, Jamison K: A comparison of outcome in adolescent and late-onset bipolar manic-depressive illness. Am J Psychiatry 134:919–922, 1977

Chess S, Thomas A, Hassibi M: Depression in childhood and adolescence: a prospective study of six cases. J Nerv Ment Dis 171:411–420, 1983

Christie KA, Burke JD, Regier DA, et al: Epidemiologic evidence for early onset of mental disorders and higher risk of drug abuse in young adults. Am J Psychiatry 145:971–975, 1988

Cohen-Sandler R, Berman AL, King RA: A follow-up study of hospitalized suicidal children. Journal of the American Academy of Child Psychiatry 21: 398–403, 1982

Coolidge JC, Brodie RD, Fenney B: A ten-year follow-up study of sixty-six school children. Am J Orthopsychiatry 34:675–684, 1964

Costello EJ, Costello AJ, Edelbrock C, et al: Psychiatric disorders in pediatric primary care: prevalence and risk factors. Arch Gen Psychiatry 45:1107–1116, 1988

Deltito JA, Perugi G, Maremmani I, et al: The importance of separation anxiety in the differentiation of panic disorder for agoraphobia. Psychiatric Developments 3:227–236, 1986

Eisenberg L: The epidemiology of suicide in adolescents. Pediatr Ann 13:47–54, 1984

Emde R, Schmidt D: The stability of children's fears. Child Dev 49:1277–1279, 1978

Flakierska N, Lindstrom M, Gillberg C: School refusal: a 15–20 year follow-up study of 35 Swedish urban children. Br J Psychiatry 152:834–837, 1988

Fowler RC, Rich CL, Young D: San Diego Suicide Study, II: substance abuse in young cases. Arch Gen Psychiatry 43:962–965, 1986

Garber J, Kriss MR, Koch M, et al: Recurrent depression in adolescents: a follow-up study. J Am Acad Child Adolesc Psychiatry 27:49–54, 1988

Gittelman R: Anxiety Disorders of Childhood. New York, Guilford, 1986

Goldacre M, Hawton K: Repetition of self-poisoning and subsequent death in adolescents who take overdoses. Br J Psychiatry 146:395–398, 1985

Harrington R, Fudge H, Rutter M, et al: Adult outcomes of childhood and adolescent depression. Arch Gen Psychiatry 47:465–473, 1990

Hayward C, Killen JD, Taylor CB: Panic attacks in young adolescents. Am J Psychiatry 146:1061–1062, 1989

Hershberg SO, Carlsen GA, Cantwell DP, et al: Anxiety and depressive disorders in psychiatrically disturbed children. J Clin Psychiatry 44:358–361, 1982

Hollingsworth CE, Tanguay PE, Grossman L, et al: Long-term outcome of obsessive-compulsive disorder in childhood. Journal of the American Academy of Child Psychiatry 19:134–144, 1980

Kandel D, Davies M: Adult sequelae of adolescent depressive symptoms. Arch Gen Psychiatry 43:255–262, 1986

Keller MB, Beardslee W, Lavori PW, et al: Course of major depression in non- referred adolescents: a retrospective study. J Affect Disord 15:235–245, 1988

Klein DF, Zifrin CM, Woerner MG, et al: Treatment of phobias, II: behavior therapy and supportive psychotherapy: are there any specific and supportive ingredients? Arch Gen Psychiatry 40:139–145, 1983

Klein RG, Last CG: Anxiety Disorders in Children. Newbury Park, CA, Sage, 1989

Klerman GL: Suicide, depression, and related problems among the baby boom cohort, in Suicide Among Youth: Perspectives on Risk and Prevention. Edited by Pfeffer CR. Washington, DC, American Psychiatric Press, 1989, pp 63–81

Klerman GL, Lavori PW, Rice J, et al: Birth-cohort trends in rates of major depressive disorder among relatives of patients with affective disorders. Arch Gen Psychiatry 42:689–693, 1985

Kolvin I, Berney P, Bhate R: Classification and diagnosis of depression in school phobia. Br J Psychiatry 145:347–357, 1984

Kovacs M, Goldston D: Cognitive and social cognitive development of depressed children and adolescents. J Am Acad Child Adolesc Psychiatry 30: 388–392, 1991

Kovacs M, Feinberg TL, Crouse-Novak A, et al: Depressive disorders in childhood, I: a longitudinal prospective study of characteristics and recovery. Arch Gen Psychiatry 41:229–237, 1984a

Kovacs M, Feinberg TL, Crouse-Novak M, et al: Depressive disorders in childhood, II: a longitudinal study of the risk for a subsequent major depression. Arch Gen Psychiatry 41:643–649, 1984b

Kovacs M, Paulauskas S, Gatsonis C, et al: Depressive disorders in childhood, III: a longitudinal study of morbidity with and risk for conduct disorders. J Affect Disord 15:205–217, 1988

Kovacs M, Gatsonis C, Paulauskas SL, et al: Depressive disorders in childhood IV. A longitudinal study of comorbidity with and risk for anxiety disorders. Arch Gen Psychiatry 46:776–782, 1989

Kuperman S, Black DW, Burns TL: Excess suicide among formerly hospitalized child psychiatry patients. J Clin Psychiatry 49:88–93, 1988

Leonard HL, Suedo SE, Rapoport JL, et al: Treatment of obsessive-compulsive disorder with clomipramine and desipramine in children and adolescents: a double-blind crossover comparison. Arch Gen Psychiatry 46:1088–1092, 1989

McGee R, Williams S: A longitudinal study of depression in nine-year-old children. J Am Acad Child Adolesc Psychiatry 27:342–348, 1988

McGee R, Freehan M, Williams S, et al: DSM-III disorders in a large sample of adolescents. J Am Acad Child Adolesc Psychiatry 29:611–619, 1990

Moreau DL, Weissman M, Warner V: Panic disorder in children at high risk for depression. Am J Psychiatry 146:1059–1060, 1989

Motto JA: Suicide in male adolescents, in Suicide in the Young. Edited by Sudak HS, Ford AB, Rushforth NB. Boston, John Wright, 1984, pp 227–244

Nardini-Maillard D, Ladane FG: The results of a follow-up study of suicidal adolescents. J Adolesc 3:253–260, 1980

National Center for Health Statistics: Advance report of final mortality statistics (1989 Monthly Vital Statistics Report 40, No 8, Suppl 2). Hyattsville, MD, Public Health Service, 1992

Otto V: Suicidal acts by children and adolescents: a follow-up study. Acta Psychiatr Scand Suppl 233:7–123, 1972

Paerregaard G: Suicide among attempted suicides: a 10-year follow-up. Suicide 5:140–144, 1975

Pergi G, Deltito J, Soriani A, et al: Relationships between panic disorder and separation anxiety with alcohol phobia. Compr Psychiatry 29:98–107, 1988

Pfeffer CR, Lipkins R, Plutchik R, et al: Normal children at risk for suicidal behavior: a two-year follow-up study. J Am Acad Child Adolesc Psychiatry 27:34–41, 1988

Pfeffer CR, Klerman GL, Hurt SW, et al: Suicidal children grow up: demographic and clinical risk factors for adolescent suicide attempts. J Am Acad Child Adolesc Psychiatry 30:609–616, 1991

Puig-Antich J: Affective disorders in childhood: a review and perspective. Psychiatr Clin North Am 3:403–424, 1980

Puig-Antich J, Lukens E, Davies M, et al: Psychosocial functioning in prepubertal major depressive disorders, I: interpersonal relationships during the depressive episode. Arch Gen Psychiatry 42:500–507, 1985a

Puig-Antich J, Lukens E, Davies M, et al: Psychosocial functioning in prepubertal major depressive disorders, II: interpersonal relationships after sustained recovery from reactive episodes. Arch Gen Psychiatry 42:511–517, 1985b

Richman N, Stevenson J, Graham PJ: Preschool to School: A Behavioral Study. London, Academic, 1982

Rodriguez A, Rodriguez M, Eisenberg L: The outcome of school phobia: a follow-up study based on 41 cases. Am J Psychiatry 116:540–544, 1959

Rutter M, Tizard J, Whitmore K: Education, Health and Behavior. New York, Krieger, 1981

Ryan ND, Puig-Antich J, Ambrosini P, et al: The clinical picture of major depression in children and adolescents. Arch Gen Psychiatry 44:854–861, 1987

Shaffer D, Garland A, Vieland V, et al: The impact of curriculum-based suicide prevention programs for teenagers. J Am Acad Child Adolesc Psychiatry 30:588–596, 1991

Stanley EJ, Barter JT: Adolescent suicidal behavior. Am J Orthopsychiatry 40:87–96, 1970

Strauss CC, Last CG, Heisen M, et al: Association between anxiety and depression in children and adolescents with anxiety disorders. J Abnorm Child Psychol 16:57–68, 1988

Strober M, Carlson G: Bipolar illness in adolescents with major depression. Arch Gen Psychiatry 39:549–555, 1982

Swedo SE, Rapoport JL: Phenomenology and differential diagnosis of obsessive-compulsive disorder in children and adolescents, in Obsessive-Compulsive Disorders in Children and Adolescents. Edited by Rapoport JL. Washington, DC, American Psychiatric Press, 1989, pp 13–32

Waldron S Jr: The significance of childhood neurosis for adult mental health: a follow-up study. Am J Psychiatry 133:532–538, 1976

Walker JL, Lahey BB, Russo MF, et al: Anxiety, inhibition, and conduct disorder in children, I: relations to social impairment. J Am Acad Child Adolesc Psychiatry 30:187–191, 1991

Weiss M, Burke A: A 5 to 10 year study follow-up of hospitalized school phobic children and adolescents. Am J Orthopsychiatry 40:672–676, 1970

Weissman MM, Klerman GL, Markowitz JS, et al: Suicidal ideation and suicide attempts in panic disorder and attacks. N Engl J Med 321:1209–1214, 1989

Welner A, Welner Z, Fishman R: Psychiatric adolescent inpatients: eight to ten year follow-up. Arch Gen Psychiatry 36:698–700, 1979

Werry JS: Overanxious disorder: a review of its taxonomic properties. J Am Acad Child Adolesc Psychiatry 30:533–544, 1991

8

Eating Disorders

Jane

She was nicknamed Lady Jane from birth, perhaps a mark of her family's expectations. The house was always in perfect order, except for the family life inside it. Her mother suicided by cutting her own throat, leaving a chilling message for the family: "This is the only way." Jane was sent away to boarding school where she worked hard, got good grades, and was absorbed in acting roles with the drama club. Behind the many roles she played was a deep sense of her own unattractiveness, which became focused on body shape and weight. An obsession with dieting led to bingeing and purging, dropping out of school, and amphetamine and alcohol abuse. A series of affairs and failed marriages continued the tragedy of her personal life, which was in sharp contrast to a skyrocketing acting career. Jane's eating disorder continued until she became pregnant.

Her pregnancy marked a turning point away from her dysphoria and her eating disorder. As she described it, "My body was literally telling me things. 'Sleep better. Eat better.' I no longer wanted coffee or cigarettes. I bought my first books on nutrition." Life seemed to become more focused after Jane took control of her diet. The successful acting career continued. She devoted herself to political activism because, for her, principles were everything. Her political activism visibly restored her battered self-esteem. Body preoccupation continued, but the new focus on physical well-being paid major dividends for her mental state. A healthy diet and vigorous exercise became her own personal program—the Jane Fonda Workout. She became a role model for millions of other women. "Getting fit is a political act," she told them. "You are truly taking charge of your life." She urged women to improve their bodies in order to become healthy in mind and spirit. Sound mind, sound body was the formula that had pulled her life together. Jane even reconciled with her father, which closed the last tangled loop in her life.

Anorexia Nervosa

The Duchess of Windsor is famous for her quip that a woman can never be too thin or too rich. Do they go together? Not really. But the rich and famous dramatically illustrate the natural history of the disease, from rock star Karen Carpenter, who died of anorexia nervosa, to ultrathin British model Twiggy, who recovered and went on to greater success as an actress. What kind of illness strikes individuals who are so bright, so educated, and so achievement oriented? Personality traits ordinarily thought to be protective against mental illness are actually risk factors for anorexia nervosa. Parents have traditionally described them as perfect children—clean, polite, well behaved, and often excellent students and athletes (Bruch 1978).

Background

For centuries, what we knew about anorexia was restricted to the anecdotal clinical experience of physicians who dealt with these young women (and occasionally, young men) who starved themselves. First described in 1686 (Morton 1720) as "nervous atrophy" from "a multitude of cares and passions of the mind," it was given its name 200 years later by Sir William Gull (1868). He attributed the disorder to the "morbid mental state" of young adolescent girls and thought he saw a family disposition. Sigmund Freud did not refer directly to the condition, although several of his patients appeared to have severe anorexia (Breuer and Freud 1893/1955). But Freud's theoretical conceptual model influenced the evolving picture of anorexia nervosa. Reconstruction of anorexic patients' developmental histories led to an entanglement of the child's wishes with the parents' in these apparently well-functioning families (Bruch 1973). Indeed, "overparenting," a kind of protectiveness that stifled the development of individuality and self-expression, became the most important factor associated with anorexia nervosa.

This profile of anorexia nervosa was based on data that did not go beyond the clinical examining room. Despite medicine's commitment to scientific objectivity and research, clinicians report individual cases more often when there is a happy outcome than when it is a discouraging one. The occurrence of anorexia nervosa in adolescent girls led to its association with puberty and the adolescent maturational process so that it became a "developmental" illness, one in which psychological conflicts over growing up ended in self-starvation. Risk factors then were puberty and the maturational drive on the one hand and opposing family influences blocking the development of individuality on the other. But which girls were most vulnerable? Stressful life situations just before the onset of anorexia, such as important losses, medical illnesses, failure at school, or moves, were identified as precipitating factors (Russell 1981).

New Directions

Understanding an illness such as anorexia nervosa requires more than a series of cases from clinical practice. It requires the study of a representative spectrum of the disease, all the way from mild, reversible cases to severe and progressively deteriorating ones. The cases of brilliant clinicians from Gull to Bruch are rich in detail but tell us little about the course of the disease in the general population. A broader view of the illness through longitudinal outcome studies is needed. Tracking down the natural course of the illness, with and without treatment, has been the research direction in the second half of the twentieth century. The purpose of this wider sweep is to develop more valid data for describing and understanding the condition. Outcome studies of the disorder have tried to identify 1) its average duration (in recovered patients), 2) the percentage of patients with a chronic course, 3) its mortality rate, 4) the effect of various treatments, and 5) the prognostic factors. But how long an observation time is required before results can be considered outcome? Which criteria should be used, and what about the importance of trusted factors such as weight, eating habits, and attitudes toward the body? How are these outcome factors to be evaluated without bias (Theander 1985)? The answers are clear. Outcome must be tracked by independent raters, not by the treating physicians. Observation time needs to be extended; a long-term disorder needs long-term follow-up before outcome can be plotted with any confidence.

Longitudinal Studies

The early outcome studies were discouraging, of course, compared with clinical case reports. Some of the previous clinical impressions were confirmed and others were not. But the studies began to distinguish the features of good outcome from poor. Hsu et al. (1979) found that poor outcome not only was associated with poor social and parental relationships in childhood, but also with an older age at onset and greater weight loss during the illness. As an important sidelight, his study confirmed "weight phobia" as the central symptom of anorexia. At follow-up, two-thirds of the patients were of normal weight yet still afraid of being "fat." To the surprise of clinicians, disturbed family relationships persisted in those who were described as recovered. Reversing these relationships was not the key to recovery.

Halmi and Falk (1982) and Halmi et al. (1979) further studied the personality traits of anorexic patients. Again, the personality traits were found to be more than premorbid traits; obsessive-compulsive symptoms persisted long after the disorder had passed. More importantly, these studies found that specific personality characteristics had a stronger association with outcome than did specific therapies.

A Swedish study of a large group of anorexic patients (Theander 1985) found that fewer than one-third had recovered and more than one-third were ill for more than 6 years. Most importantly, the study found a distinct relationship between anorexia nervosa and affective disorder, confirming what clinicians had suspected for years. Underlying psychopathology was becoming better defined. Depression, anxiety, and obsessive-compulsive traits were intimately linked to the illness and were found to persist years after recovery. Recent longitudinal studies suggest that young adults with anorexia nervosa that began in adolescence frequently have obsessive-compulsive disorder (OCD) and avoidant personality disorder as well (Gillberg et al. 1995).

A group of researchers in Copenhagen (Tolstrup et al. 1985) followed a large sample of patients for more than 10 years. Half were found to be healthy and well-functioning regardless of treatment (none versus medical versus psychiatric). But when anorexia assumed a chronic course, it caused varying degrees of permanent impairment of function in one or more spheres of life. Unexpected was the finding that even the so-called recovered group experienced a significant decline in social functioning.

In a subsequent review, the authors of the Swedish study (Theander 1985) summarized what was known to date from longitudinal studies: the longer the follow-up, the more patients recovered and the more patients died. After 10 years, only a few still had the disorder alone, but most had other problems, both medical and psychological. The work by Theander (1985) also set common criteria for improvement: regular menstruation, stable body weight, reasonable eating habits, and a realistic conception of body size. Other studies have shown that after 6 or 7 years 1) most anorexia nervosa subjects no longer met the criteria for the disorder, but many continued to meet the criteria for other eating disorders; 2) there was a high rate of OCD; and 3) affective disorders tended to follow the course of the eating disorder rather than precede or postdate it (Rastam et al. 1995).

As cross-national studies became more common, standards were necessary for investigators using clinical assessments. The key, of course, was a comparison group of nonanorexic women so that baseline parameters, ranging from body satisfaction to social adjustment, could be measured and evaluated. The work of Canadian researchers using such a control group (Toner et al. 1986) confirmed the previously found association of affective disorder with anorexia, this time using DSM-III (American Psychiatric Association 1980) criteria. In other words, compared with the number of women of average weight, significantly more women with anorexia nervosa met DSM-III criteria for affective/anxiety disorder at long-term follow-up.

What Have We Learned?

Favorable prognostic signs have become better defined by these long-term follow-up studies: earlier onset, shorter illness, less severe weight loss, continued perception of hunger, better family relationships, and uninterrupted school or work history. Unfavorable prognostic factors include bulimia associated with the anorexia, severe weight loss, more frequent hospital admissions, and severe disturbances in body image.

However, even good outcome means continued problems for most. Recovered anorexic patients show distorted attitudes toward eating,
weight, and food (Clinton and McKinley 1986; Hall et al. 1984). Most
continue diet restrictions and consider themselves overweight (Kaye et
al. 1986). Many also show some sign of psychiatric impairment, most often chronic depression (Nuusbaum et al. 1985).

The natural history of anorexia nervosa appears to range from 1)
permanent recovery with or without sequelae to 2) a chronic course to 3)
a downhill course, including untimely death. After 5 years, the outcome
of the disorder roughly follows the rule of thirds: approximately
one-third of anorexic patients are relatively symptom free, one-third
have symptoms but are functioning, and one-third are incapacitated.
But categorization by outcome subgroups (Theander 1983) does not tell
the whole story. Mortality rate ranges from 5% to 10%, averaging 1.5%
per year. The disorder is a serious one.

Bulimia Nervosa

Much less is known about anorexia's sister illness, bulimia nervosa. Its status as an illness is only a few years old, and long-term studies are lacking.

Bulimia was recognized as a symptom at the turn of the century by
Osler (1892) and Janet (1903). By the 1960s, bulimia had become identified in fully half of anorexic patients (Casper 1983). Efforts to establish a
prevalence pattern for bulimia in the general population resulted in
seemingly very high rates (Halmi et al. 1981), leading to media reports of
an epidemic of bulimia among college-age women. However, these
studies were based on bulimia symptoms from self-report questionnaires drawn from a narrow age and social-class range, which blurred
the focus on the development of a condition with specific criteria for
caseness. First described as a discrete illness in Britain by Russell (1979),
the future of bulimia nervosa was assured by DSM-III-R (American Psychiatric Association 1987), which identified its specific criteria as persistent overconcern with body shape and weight. Bulimia nervosa now
appears to affect 1%–2% of high school– and college-age females,
whereas 5%–15% report bulimic symptoms (Bushnell et al. 1990). Because of bulimia's recent debut as an illness, the pinpointing of its course
as accurately as that in anorexia nervosa is premature. But what is
known for certain?

There are three main findings. First of all, there is a moderately high frequency of crossover between anorexia nervosa and bulimia nervosa in both directions, suggesting an important connection between them (Herzog et al. 1988). Second, preliminary follow-up data (Hsu and Sobkiewicz 1989) suggest that bulimia nervosa will have a pattern similar to anorexia nervosa; that is, some patients will continue to be ill at follow-up, whereas others apparently will have recovered. Third, affective disorder is more common among those with bulimia nervosa who do not improve, just as with those who have anorexia nervosa. Indeed, some come to a tentative conclusion that the worst outcome is associated with depression combined with anorexia nervosa combined with bulimia nervosa (Sohlberg et al. 1989).

Conclusions

What is known about the outcome of the eating disorders? More is known about the outcome of anorexia nervosa than bulimia nervosa. Longitudinal studies have confirmed clinical experience that the course of eating disorders can be completely reversible in some young women, chronic in others, and fatal in a few. At highest risk for severe outcome are those whose illness begins at an older age and when the anorexia is combined with bulimia, when the weight loss is extreme, when attitudes toward food and weight are bizarre, and when the illness has a longer duration. These negative signs (and their opposite positive signs—early onset, shorter duration, minor weight loss, good family relationships, and social adjustment) have a stronger association with outcome than any treatment intervention. This fact is startling. The prognosis in anorexia has not improved because standard treatment approaches have not replaced the theoretical formulations and techniques used by clinicians over the centuries. Nevertheless, some previously held, if fragile, clinical impressions have been confirmed as important prognostic features. Anorexic patients with hysterical personality traits have been found to have a more favorable prognosis than those who have obsessive-compulsive traits, perhaps suggesting that it is easier to outgrow an illness that is more psychosocial than biological ("soft" versus "hard" anorexia). Those patients with a higher level of psychosexual maturity, heterosexual interest, and/or a functional marriage are better off. So are those with an internal rather than external locus of control (Santonastaso et al. 1987), confirming the belief that a sense of helplessness and ineffectiveness is, if not universal, an important feature for more serious prognosis. The loop between childhood and adulthood is not yet closed. A study of a large, random sample population found that certain early eating habits were predictive of anorexia nervosa (Marchi and Cohen 1990). The circle will be closed if the future anorexic college student can be recognized in the toddler picking at her food in the high chair.

There is no question that large group follow-up studies are generally less encouraging than are individual case reports. But this is a scientific era—an era of facts rather than an era of ideas—and facts are inevitably more discouraging than theories. Although the focus has shifted from the internal psychodynamic issues to the external descriptive factors, their meaning is unclear. For example, it is now known that eating disorders are more common in sisters and mothers of patients than in the general population (American Psychiatric Association 1994). A population-based study of female twins supports the notion of a spectrum of anorexic-like syndromes in women, which are familial and share familial etiological factors with major depression and bulimia nervosa (Walters and Kendler 1995). The concept of genetic loading may be replacing the sacred family patterns associated with eating disorders. Yet family interactions and child-rearing practices are still critical risk factors that are more important in some cases than in others. They are simply more difficult to measure by today's scientific standards.

Generalizing from individual cases to the population at large must be done cautiously because statistical studies do not indicate what will happen to the individual patient. The course of illness can be only superficially understood by rating instruments. One of the mysteries of anorexia nervosa is the unpredictability of the prognosis in individuals (Russell 1977). Vulnerability is an individual matter. Eating disorders may form a spectrum, ranging from normal eating and a lack of concern about weight to moderately dysregulated eating and a normal concern about weight, and from impaired function to more serious mental and physical illness due to bulimia nervosa or anorexia nervosa.

References

American Psychiatric Association: Diagnostic and Statistical Manual of Mental Disorders, 3rd Edition. Washington, DC, American Psychiatric Association, 1980

American Psychiatric Association: Diagnostic and Statistical Manual of Mental Disorders, 3rd Edition, Revised. Washington, DC, American Psychiatric Association, 1987

Breuer J, Freud S: Studies on hysteria (1893–1895), in The Standard Edition of the Complete Psychological Works of Sigmund Freud, Vol. 2. Translated and edited by Strachey J. London, Hogarth Press, 1955, pp 201–319

Bruch H: Eating Disorders: Obesity and Anorexia Nervosa and the Person Within. New York, Basic Books, 1973

Bruch H: The Golden Cage: The Enigma of Anorexia Nervosa. Cambridge, MA, Harvard University Press, 1978

Bushnell JA, Wells JE, Hornblow AR, et al: Prevalence of three bulimia syndromes in the general population. Psychol Med 20:671–680, 1990

Casper RC: On the emergence of bulimia nervosa as a syndrome: a historical review. Int J Eat Disord 2:316, 1983

Clinton DM, McKinley WW: Attitudes to food, eating and weight in acutely ill and recovered anorectics. Br J Clin Psychol 25:61–67, 1986

Gillberg IC, Rastam M, Gillberg C: Anorexia nervosa 6 years after onset, I: personality disorders. Compr Psychiatry 36:61–69, 1995

Gull W: The address on medicine. Lancet 2:171–176, 1868

Hall A, Slim E, Hawker F, et al: Anorexia nervosa: long-term outcome in 50 female patients. Br J Psychiatry 145:407–413, 1984

Halmi K, Falk JR: Anorexia nervosa: a study of outcome discriminators in exclusive dieters and bulimics. J Am Acad Child Adolesc Psychiatry 21:369–375, 1982

Halmi K, Goldberg S, Casper R, et al: Pretreatment predictors of outcome in anorexia nervosa. Br J Psychiatry 134:71–78, 1979

Halmi KA, Falk JR, Schwartz E: Binge eating and vomiting: a survey of a college population. Psychol Med 11:697–706, 1981

Herzog DB, Keller MB, Lavori PW: Outcome in anorexia nervosa and bulimia nervosa: a review of the literature. J Nerv Ment Dis 176:131–143, 1988

Hsu LKG, Sobkiewicz TA: Bulimia nervosa: a four- to six-year follow-up study. Psychol Med 19:1035–1038, 1989

Hsu LKG, Crisp AH, Harding B: Outcome of anorexia. Lancet 1:61–65, 1979

Janet P: Obsessions et la Psychasthenie, Vols 1 and 2. Paris, Felix Alcan, 1903

Kaye WH, Gwirtsman H, George T, et al: Caloric consumption and activity levels after weight recovery in anorexia nervosa: a prolonged delay in normalization. Int J Eat Disord 5:489–502, 1986

Marchi M, Cohen P: Early childhood eating behaviors and adolescent eating disorders. J Am Acad Child Adolesc Psychiatry 29:112–117, 1990

Morton R: Phthisiologia or, A Treatise of Consumptions, 2nd Edition. London, Smith, 1720

Nuusbaum M, Shenker IR, Baird D, et al: Follow-up investigation in patients with anorexia nervosa. J Pediatr 106:835–840, 1985

Osler W: Principles and Practice of Medicine. New York, D Appleton, 1892

Rastam M, Gillberg IC, Gillberg C: Anorexia nervosa 6 years after onset, II: comorbid psychiatric problems. Compr Psychiatry 36:70–76, 1995

Russell G: The current treatment of anorexia nervosa. Br J Psychiatry 138:164–166, 1981

Russell G: Bulimia nervosa: an ominous variant of anorexia nervosa. Psychol Med 9:429–448, 1979

Santonastaso P, Favaretto G, Canton G: Anorexia nervosa in Italy: clinical features and outcome in a long-term follow-up study. Psychopathology 20:8–17, 1987

Sohlberg S, Norring C, Holmgren S, et al: Impulsivity and long-term prognosis of psychiatric patients with anorexia nervosa/bulimia nervosa. J Nerv Ment Dis 177:249–258, 1989

Theander S: Research on outcome and prognosis of anorexia nervosa and some results from a Swedish long-term study. Int J Eat Disord 2:167–174, 1983

Theander S: Outcome and prognosis in anorexia nervosa and bulimia: some results of previous investigations compared with those of a Swedish long-term study. J Psychiatr Res 19:493–508, 1985

Tolstrup K, Brinch M, Isager T, et al: Long-term outcome of 151 cases of anorexia nervosa (the Copenhagen Anorexia Nervosa Follow-up Study). Acta Psychiatr Scand 71:380–387, 1985

Toner B, Garfinkel P, Garner D: Long-term follow-up of anorexia nervosa. Psychosom Med 48:520–529, 1986

Walters EE, Kendler KS: Anorexia nervosa and anorexic-like syndromes in a population-based female twin sample. Am J Psychiatry 152:64–71, 1995

9

Attention-Deficit/ Hyperactivity Disorder

John

John was first seen in consultation when he was 3 years old on referral from his pediatrician. The pre-, peri-, and postnatal history was negative for any physical insult, and he was a "healthy baby." However, as an infant, he was irritable and could not be soothed. His sleep pattern was erratic and he did not sleep for any length of time. He wiggled all the time. At age 4 months, he was attempting to pull himself up to a standing position. At age 7 months, he was trying to walk and at 8 months he was a "runner." He was not well-coordinated and had frequent accidents, falling and bumping into furniture. His parents described him as hyperactive, impulsive, and distractible, with a short attention span, low frustration tolerance, and emotional lability. Although he was friendly, outgoing, and liked other children, they were wary of him because in his eagerness to be friends he would rush toward them, often grabbing or bowling them over. In a shopping mall, he was overstimulated and would run off. He was not afraid of being lost. John, at age 3 years, slept about 5–6 hours at night. He would wake up and wander through the house, "make a mess in the kitchen," or wake up his parents or siblings. His preschool teacher said that he could not continue to attend the school unless something were done to decrease his impulsivity.

John's father said that John reminded him of himself when he was a child. Also, the brother of John's father had a son who was diagnosed as having attention-deficit/hyperactivity disorder (ADHD) and who responded to stimulant medication. John's parents had read some literature on ADHD and recognized the need for structure and consistency with John. They did not have any difficulty with John's older brother and sister.

John's pediatrician had prescribed an antihistamine for his condition, but his improvement was modest. In the initial consultation, his parents were given specific recommendations on behavioral management techniques and techniques to implement a structured parenting approach. Also, a preschool program that had fewer children and a structured approach was recommended.

John continued to exhibit ADHD signs and, when he was age 5 years and in kindergarten, stimulant medication was prescribed. He responded to the medication. In succeeding years, attempts were made to discontinue or decrease the medication without success. In fact, it had to be increased, but he did not develop side effects. He did not have a learning disability nor did he develop a conduct disorder. Periodically he would be "stubborn" but did not develop all the signs of an oppositional defiant disorder.

In junior high school, he had difficulty because he now was changing classes every hour and could not "settle down." He had difficulty concentrating on homework, and he required medication to help him concentrate when he did homework. John was well coordinated and enjoyed sports. He was social and gracious, but he often "talked too much" in class. In high school, he did not want his peers to know he was taking medication, so the long-acting preparation of the stimulant was prescribed and he continued to benefit from the medication.

John had both hyperactivity and a short attention span. Like many children with ADHD, he developed symptoms at an early age, and they continued into high school. Again, like many hyperactive boys, he had a father who had had similar problems as a child. John's symptoms were alleviated to some extent by stimulant medication, but it was found necessary to continue the medication through high school. Although the symptoms of hyperactivity and short attention span were once thought almost always to decrease with age, in some cases they do not, so that even as adults these people benefit from taking medication.

Epidemiology and Course

Two books, one by Barkley (1990) and one by Weiss and Hechtman (1986), provide comprehensive reviews of the ADHD literature. This chapter focuses on longitudinal studies of the condition.

Gittelman et al. (1985) found that 31% of their study group had attention-deficit disorder with hyperactivity that persisted into adult life and a higher incidence of conduct and substance abuse disorders than control subjects. Follow-up studies indicate that 30%–50% of ADHD cases continue into adulthood. ADHD appears to lead to increased psychopathology and antisocial outcome in about 25% of adults.

Barkley et al. (1990) reported an 8-year follow-up study of 1,234 hyperactive children and 66 healthy control subjects into adolescence. More than 80% of the hyperactive children had ADHD, and 60% had either oppositional defiant disorder and/or conduct disorder at outcome. Cigarette and/or marijuana use and negative academic outcomes were significantly higher in the ADHD group. The pattern of symptoms was found to be stable over time and associated with greater risk for family disturbance, as well as negative academic and social outcomes in adolescence. Substantially greater numbers of hyperactive subjects were found to have negative outcomes than in previous studies. The evidence of psychopathology was similar, 71%–84%, in the Mendelson et al. (1971) retrospective study. Conduct disorder was 43% at follow-up, similar to 45% in the Gittelman et al. (1985) sample. Substance abuse appeared to be associated with conduct disorder in hyperactive subjects (Gittelman et al. 1985). Purely hyperactive subjects did not have higher cigarette, alcohol, or drug use compared with control subjects, but hyperactive subjects with conduct disorders had rates of cigarette and marijuana use that were two to three times greater than alcohol use. Conduct disorder appeared to mediate the development of substance use in hyperactive adolescents. Conduct disorder did not appear to increase the risk for grade failure, but the presence of hyperactivity did; pure hyperactive subjects and those with conduct disorder had similar rates that were three times greater than that of the control group. Conduct disorder increased the risk for school suspension, expulsion, and school dropout rates.

Barkley (1990) summarized adult outcome studies. ADHD children in adulthood have problems with behavior in general, and 50%–65% continue to have ADHD symptoms. Twenty to 45% have some antisocial behavior, with about 25% qualifying for the diagnosis of antisocial personality disorder. They have more problems with self-esteem than do non-ADHD adults. Barkley (1990) emphasized the need to consider a combination of variables: family socioeconomic status (SES), childhood intelligence and aggression, poor parental management techniques, parent psychiatric disturbance, and family dysfunction. He noted that the best outcome is associated with milder ADHD symptoms, higher intelligence, well-adjusted parents, and stable family environment. In general, the majority of ADHD children as adults satisfactorily adjust to their symptoms.

IQ, low initial aggressivity, and low initial antisocial behavior appear to be important factors for good outcome of ADHD. IQ appears to be important for academic achievement, and low initial aggression in childhood is important for a low incidence of later adult aggression, as well as for good overall adolescent and adult functioning.

Predictive Factors

Predictive family factors have been studied by several investigators (Loney et al. 1981; Mendelson et al. 1971; Minde et al. 1972; Stewart et al. 1979; Weiss et al. 1971). Children who were unsocialized/aggressive tended to have fathers who were antisocial. Poor mental health of the parents, coupled with poor mother-child relationship and punitive child-rearing practices, predicted overt antisocial behavior in adolescence. Long-term outcome was more positive for subjects whose parents were consistent and firm and respected the children (Werner and Smith 1977). In adolescence, family factors as well as achievement enter into the prediction of aggressive, hyperactive, and delinquent behavior.

Predictive factors pertaining to treatment are somewhat difficult to evaluate because the subjects who often had the most interventions were those who had the greatest difficulties and often, on follow-up, were the least improved. Also, the specific interventions sometimes are not described in sufficient detail. The group that received more psychiatric treatment was more aggressive and distractible on initial assessment (Minde et al. 1972). An extensive review of the efficacy of remedial programs for children with learning disabilities showed that few studies found long-term benefits from the programs (Helper 1980). A 25-year retrospective follow-up study of 18 hyperactive patients who received supportive treatment and more appropriate school placement concluded that there was no correlation between outcome and the amount of help the subjects received (Menkes et al. 1967). Some studies concluded that psychotherapy, counseling, and remedial help are not particularly predictive of long-term outcome in hyperactive children. The problem in assessing the long-term impact is that those requiring the interventions have more problems to begin with and are more likely to have a poorer outcome. Well-controlled studies with matched subjects have yet to be done.

Studies on the long-term effect of stimulant drug treatment have been reported (Conrad and Insel 1967; Loney et al. 1975; Weiss et al. 1975). Long-term treatment in childhood did not significantly affect hyperactive adolescents' outcome, but if the subjects were taking stimulant medication and had a good family situation, there was a significant correlation with good outcome as judged by academic achievement, emotional adjustment, and absence of delinquency. There appears to be an interaction between family factors and medication. The majority of studies of treatment with medication alone have shown an absence of long-term improvement when assessed in adolescence. However, most studies support the need for a comprehensive, multimodal treatment approach, combining medication, special education, parent counseling and training in child management, individual therapy, and classroom consultation (Satterfield et al. 1981). If this approach continued for several years, the program improved the prognosis for ADHD children, especially those with aggression. However, Gittelman et al. (1980) randomly assigned 61 ADHD subjects to three treatment groups. Groups receiving methylphenidate and behavior modification therapy or methylphenidate alone did better than the group receiving behavior modification alone. Most researchers tend to believe that a combination of behavior therapy and medication is the best approach to the treatment of ADHD (Pelham and Murphy 1986). This finding is supported by a study (Feldman et al. 1979) of 81 hyperactive subjects as adolescents and 48 hyperactive subjects as adults. Only 8% of the adolescents and 10% of the adults had serious problems. The positive outcome was attributed to the fact that they received comprehensive treatment in a multidisciplinary setting. Weiss and Hechtman (1986) noted that, as young adults, adolescents who had received stimulant treatment previously usually got along better with co-workers than did the untreated hyperactive subjects. Control subjects were seen as working more independently. Compared with a control group, the stimulant-treated hyperactive subjects had more difficulties with aggression. However, the untreated group had even more difficulties with aggression and antisocial behavior in the past year, with stealing, and with using alcohol and nonmedical drugs. Stimulant-treated hyperactive subjects seemed to do better than the untreated hyperactive subjects as adults in several areas: fewer car accidents, seeing their childhood more positively, better social skills and self-esteem, fewer problems with aggression, and less need for current psychiatric treatment. Stimulant treatment of hyperactive subjects in childhood may not eliminate educational, work, and life difficulties, but it may result in less social ostracism, with hyperactive subjects having better feelings toward themselves and others.

Weiss and Hechtman's book (1986) is a follow-up study of ADHD children as young adults that includes extensive reviews of the significant literature. The authors caution that associations made between initial factors and adult outcomes do not prove causality. However, certain predictive variables stand out: SES and mental health of family members. IQ enters almost every outcome measure and is particularly important in educational achievement and nonmedical drug use. Weiss and Hechtman (1986) stress the role of aggressivity, emotional instability, and low frustration tolerance in influencing outcome.

Wallender and Hubert (1985), in an extensive review of the literature, concluded that young adults with ADHD had employment histories and work ratings comparable to those of control subjects. These young adults also had more car accidents, lower self-esteem, less socializing, and more restlessness. The authors observed that although adult adjustment to ADHD, which frequently is ostensibly normal, may be better than is predicted from childhood and adolescent functioning, there may be differences between young adults with ADHD and their peers without ADHD.

Childhood intelligence, hyperactivity, child-rearing practices, SES of parents, and emotional stability in the home interact to predict academic achievement. Childhood antisocial behavior is associated with an increased number of firings from jobs, and childhood aggression is associated with increased likelihood of criminal activities in adult life. Factors that contribute to a lesser degree of criminal activity in adult life are associated with several childhood factors: IQ, hyperactivity, SES, mental health of family members, and emotional climate in the home.

No single factor in childhood predicts adult adjustment of ADHD children. However, the significant associated factors appear to be intelligence, minimal aggression, emotional stability in childhood, family environment, and child-rearing practices of the parents. In John's case, discussed at the beginning of this chapter, his parents sought treatment for him at an early age and John had a winning personality, both of which may have played a major role in successful outcome.

References

Barkley RA: Attention-Deficit Hyperactivity Disorder: A Handbook for Diagnosis and Treatment. New York, Guilford, 1990

Barkley RA, Fischer M, Edelbrock CS, et al: The adolescent outcome of hyperactive children diagnosed by research criteria, I: an 8-year prospective follow-up study. J Am Acad Child Adolesc Psychiatry 29:546–557, 1990

Conrad WG, Insel J: Anticipating the response to amphetamine therapy in the treatment of hyperkinetic children. Pediatrics 40:96–98, 1967

Feldman S, Denhoff E, Denhoff J: The attention disorder and related syndromes: outcome in adolescence and young adult life, in Minimal Brain Dysfunction: A Developmental Approach. Edited by Stern L, Denhoff E. New York, Mason Publishing, 1979

Gittelman R, Abkoff H, Pollack E, et al: A controlled trial of behavior modification and methylphenidate in hyperactive children, in Hyperactive Children: The Social Ecology of Identification and Treatment. Edited by Whalen C, Henker B. New York, Academic Press, 1980, pp 221–246

Gittelman R, Mannuzza S, Shenker S: Hyperactive boys almost grown up. Arch Gen Psychiatry 42:937–947, 1985

Helper M: Follow-up of children with minimal brain dysfunctions: outcome and predictors, in Handbook of Minimal Brain Dysfunction: A Critical Review. Edited by Rie HE, Rie ER. New York, John Wiley & Sons, 1980

Loney J, Comly HH, Siemon B: Parental management, self-concept, and drug response. Journal of Learning Disabilities 8:187–190, 1975

Loney J, Whaley-Klahn M, Kosier T, et al: Hyperactive boys and their brothers at 21: predictors of aggressive and antisocial outcomes. Paper presented at a meeting of the Society for Life History Research, Monterey, CA, November 1981

Mendelson WB, Johnson NE, Stewart MA: Hyperactive children as teenagers: a follow-up study. J Nerv Ment Dis 153:273–279, 1971

Menkes MM, Rowe JS, Menkes JH: A twenty-five year follow-up study on the hyperactive child with minimal brain dysfunction. Pediatrics 39:393–399, 1967

Minde K, Weiss G, Mendelson N: A five-year follow up study of 91 hyperactive school children. Journal of the American Academy of Child Psychiatry 11: 595–610, 1972

Pelham WE, Murphy HA: Attention deficit and conduct disorders, in Pharmacological and Behavioral Treatments: An Integrative Approach. Edited by Hersow M. New York, Wiley, 1986, pp 108–148

Satterfield JH, Satterfield BH, Cantwell DP: Three-year multimodality treatment study of 100 hyperactive boys. J Pediatr 98:650–655, 1981

Stewart MA, de Blois CS, Singer S: Alcoholism and hyperactivity revisited. Currents in Alcoholism 5:349–357, 1979

Wallender JL, Hubert NC: Long-term prognosis for children with attention deficit disorder with hyperactivity (ADD/H). Advances in Clinical Child Psychology 8:113–147, 1985

Weiss G, Hechtman LT: Hyperactive Children Grown Up. New York, Guilford, 1986

Weiss G, Minde K, Werry JS, et al: Studies on the hyperactive child, VIII: five-year follow-up. Arch Gen Psychiatry 24:409–414, 1971

Weiss G, Kruger E, Danielson U, et al: Effects of long-term treatment of hyperactive children with methylphenidate. Canadian Medical Association Journal 112:159–165, 1975

Werner E, Smith R: Kauai's Children Come of Age. Honolulu, University of Hawaii Press, 1977

10

Conduct Disorder

Carl

Carl was referred for evaluation because his mother complained that he was "stubborn," did not mind her, hit other children, and was aggressive. His father believed that Carl was "all boy" and stated that Carl's mother was too lenient in her discipline and that Carl would outgrow any difficulties he had now. His father thought that eventually Carl would see "who was the boss," since he believed consistent spanking would change Carl's behavior, although there was little "wrong" in what Carl did now.

The psychiatrist recommended therapy for Carl and counseling for his parents. The father attended two sessions to please Carl's mother but said it was a waste of time and refused to return. When seen alone, Carl's mother said that her husband demeaned her, sometimes hit her "but not too hard," and as a boy had engaged in delinquent behavior. As a youth, Carl's father had been apprehended for breaking and entering and had been imprisoned for a year. He also drank excessively and became "mean" when drunk. She thought of leaving him but stayed in the marriage for economic reasons. She was afraid she could not manage if she were alone. Meanwhile, Carl showed modest improvement in therapy, but his mother discontinued therapy under pressure from his father.

When Carl entered school, his teachers viewed him as oppositional and disobedient. He was evaluated for learning disabilities, but none was found. At age 8 years, he was classified as emotionally impaired because of acting-out behavior and was placed in a special class.

He consistently tried to boss his peers and modeled himself after older boys who were "tough." He wanted to be seen as tough, too, and when he was age 10, he began to be truant from school and to steal. Repeated attempts at counseling were unsuccessful, and at age 12 years he was placed in a group home under court supervision. He returned home at age 14 and within a year was apprehended for repeated breaking and entering. With a reputation for aggressive, risk-taking behavior, he was remanded to a training school for delinquent boys and then to a group home. As a young adult, he was charged with assault and battery, convicted, and given a jail sentence. He was diagnosed as having antisocial personality disorder by the court clinic.

Carl's history illustrates many of the features seen in individuals diagnosed in childhood with conduct disorder. Many children with conduct disturbance do not go on to be criminals, but their risk of later delinquency and school failure is high.

Carl's symptoms began early in life. It is possible that his aggressive behavior was contributed to by biological or neurological factors and that this behavior was inherited as a temperamental trait. Unquestionably, Carl's aggression was reinforced and magnified by his father's encouragement. Not only did his father dismiss and excuse Carl's misbehavior, but he also represented to Carl a role model who had been delinquent as a youth and aggressive and abusive to his wife. Carl received little help during early childhood, at a time when therapy might have been effective. His bullying of other children must have made him unpopular and may have reinforced his defiance of others, a cycle of social failures that further marginalizes a child and diminishes his or her opportunities for corrective experiences. Carl became delinquent before junior high school and was placed in a group home, where his peer role models also may have been delinquent or troubled. He remained violent as a young adult and eventually went to jail.

Epidemiological, Genetic, and Risk Factor Studies

A report from the Institute of Medicine (1989) notes that the prevalence of conduct disorder in children is from 2% to 6%. The rate is estimated to be 6.5% in boys ages 4–11 years and 10.5% in boys ages 12–16 years. For girls at the same ages, the rates are 1.8% and 4.1%, respectively.

The genetic contribution to conduct disorder has been investigated in studies of twins and adopted children. There is a greater concordance of criminality and antisocial behavior in monozygotic compared with dizygotic twins (Cloninger et al. 1978). Criminal and antisocial behavior is greater in adoptees when the biological parents have exhibited similar behavior (Cadoret 1978). However, most investigators concur that genetic and environmental factors interact; the risk for conduct disorder is greatly increased when both genetic and environmental factors are present (Cadoret et al. 1983; Cloninger et al. 1982; Mednick and Hutchings 1978).

What risk factors predict conduct disorder (Glueck and Glueck 1959; Mitchell and Rosa 1981; Rutsma-Street et al. 1985)? Boyle and Offord (1990) found that conduct disorder is significantly associated with being raised by a single parent. This finding does not exclude genetic or environmental factors because absent fathers are less likely to be optimally functioning themselves, and single mothers are more likely to be struggling with bills and discipline. Kazdin (1986) has summarized the risk factors for conduct disorder continuing into adulthood as antisocial behavior. Significant risks are early onset of antisocial behavior (before ages 10–12 years) and a history of many and different types of antisocial behavior in various settings. Behaviors such as aggression, truancy, impulsiveness, stealing, and oppositional behavior indicate greater risk for adult antisocial behavior. Parental antisocial behavior, parental alcoholism, unemployment, poor supervision of the child, inconsistent discipline, marital discord, abuse, and large family size are all factors that both contribute to childhood conduct disorder and predict adult antisocial behavior.

The more risk factors, the greater the risk of conduct disorder: a cascade effect. In the face of a large number of risk factors, even intellectual ability, usually a positive variable, is not a powerful protective factor. However, a study of 12 schools (Rutter et al. 1979) found that teacher and school characteristics positively or negatively influenced children's school attendance, behavior, delinquency rates, and academic performance.

Quay (1987) drew the following seven conclusions from a survey of predictors of delinquency:

1. Early conduct problems are predictive of delinquency, including serious delinquency, and in some cases, of recidivism.
2. Young adolescents who are still aggressive are at a high risk for delinquency and continued aggressive behavior.

3. Committing serious juvenile offenses is a predictor of continued delinquency in adulthood.
4. Family variables, poor supervision, and parents' rejection of the
   child are strong predictors. Lack of discipline, lack of involvement,
   parents' criminality, aggression, and marital discord are moderately
   strong predictors.
5. Poor educational performance is associated with conduct disorder;
   however, there is disagreement about whether this poor performance is cause or effect.
6. Conduct problems in elementary school predict eventual chronic
   offenders.
7. Highly aggressive children more often become violent delinquents.

Although academic and intellectual functioning are associated with
other variables such as socioeconomic status (SES) and family size, when
SES and family size are controlled, academic and intellectual functioning predict antisocial behavior. West (1982) concluded that presence of
any one of the following five factors doubled the likelihood of a child's
being delinquent: 1) below average IQ, 2) low family income, 3) large
family (five or more siblings by the child's 10th birthday), 4) parents who
in the judgment of the investigator performed child-rearing duties un-
satisfactorily, and 5) a parent with a criminal record (this factor was the
most powerful predictor).

Certain characteristics of parents place children at risk for conduct
disorder. Parents' criminal behavior and alcoholism are only two factors
(Rutter and Giller 1983), but they are strong and consistent factors. If
parents were school truants and dropped out of high school, their children were at risk for the same behavior and conduct disorder (Robins
1978). Robins also noted that the prognosis is poor for children with conduct disorder: 50% of conduct disorder children referred to clinics will
become adults with antisocial behavior. Additionally, fathers' degree of
aggression as children correlates well with level of aggression in their
children (Huesmann et al. 1984).

A number of additional parent-child factors have been associated
with conduct disorder. Harsh discipline (Farrington 1978; Glueck and
Glueck 1968), abuse of the child and spouse (Behar and Stewart 1982;
Lewis et al. 1983), lax and inconsistent discipline (Glueck and Glueck
1950; W. McCord et al. 1959), poor supervision and absence of consistent
rules (Glueck and Glueck 1968; Robins 1966; H. Wilson 1980), and less
parental acceptance, warmth, affection, emotional support, and attach-

ment (Locher and Dishion 1984) have all been found to be associated with development of conduct disturbance.

Chronic marital discord, interpersonal conflict, and aggression in parental relationships also have been implicated as risk factors for development of conduct disorders in children (Hetherington and Martin 1979; Rutter and Giller 1983). Severity of marital discord appears to be the most significant factor.

Social Class and Conduct Disorder

More children with conduct disorders are in the lower socioeconomic class than the middle and upper classes; this finding is compounded by the fact that members of the lower socioeconomic class, in general, are from larger families, live in overcrowded households, and are poorly supervised. Social class and property are not powerful factors for conduct disorder if family size, overcrowding, and poor supervision are controlled for in studies of conduct disorder. When family income and household quarters are adequate, family size is less of a risk factor (West 1982).

Outcome Without Treatment

One of the earliest reports on outcome of conduct disorder without treatment was by Robins (1966). It is also one of the most frequently cited studies on the adult outcome of childhood conduct disorders. Five hundred child guidance clinic patients were compared with 100 nonpatient children. Eighty-two percent of the subjects were interviewed as adults and official records were obtained on 98%. By every measure, as adults, those with conduct disorder were significantly more disturbed than subjects who had other diagnoses in childhood. As adults, the conduct disorder patients had higher arrest rates, had fewer full-time jobs, were hospitalized more, were more socially alienated, had higher rates of alcohol abuse, and reported feeling ill more frequently.

The results of a long-term follow-up of 200 subjects by Cass and Thomas (1979) were similar to Robins' (1966) results. Other follow-up studies at 4 years (Wodarski 1979), 18 years (Faretra 1981), and 25 years (W. McCord and Sanchez 1983) also have reported poor outcomes of various forms of treatment in children with conduct disorder or delinquent youths.

Robins (1979) concluded that "antisocial personality seems to be a real syndrome in American males, one that rarely occurs in the absence of serious antisocial behavior in childhood" (p. 232).

At the time of Robins' work, conduct disorder was differentiated between two subtypes: *socialized* (youths whose antisocial behaviors were learned from those in their environment but who nonetheless were capable of empathy and attachment) and *undersocialized* (youths who were exploitative, unattached, and incapable of empathy). Robins observed differences in childhood behaviors related to undersocialized as compared with socialized conduct disorder. Henn et al. (1980) found that the youngsters with undersocialized conduct disorder did not adjust well in an institutional setting and were resistant to change. Quay (1986) noted that conduct disorder, especially the undersocialized type, shows considerable persistence from childhood to adulthood. Individuals who were found to be offenders as adults had conduct disorder as children and adolescents.

Outcome With Treatment

Two reviews in the 1970s (Lipton et al. 1975; J. A. McCord 1978) concluded that treatment of conduct disorder, whether in community, residential, or institutional settings, was not effective. In contrast to earlier treatment studies, which were pessimistic about the effects of treatment, findings from more recent studies offer hope that the course of conduct disorder is not immutable.

Several pioneering treatment programs have reported a degree of success. The California Community Treatment Program (Palmer 1974) initially was based on nonresidential treatment. Later, in recognition of the fact that 25%–35% of the youths did not respond to the community intervention program, a residential treatment program was added. On 18-month follow-up, those in residential treatment had a 58% rearrest rate versus a 94% rearrest rate for those who had initially been judged to need residential treatment but did not receive it. There were also significant differences between the two groups in number of offenses on follow-up. Palmer suggested that delinquent behavior can probably be reduced with community and residential programs if there is careful diagnosis and placement in appropriate programs.

Jesness (1975) reported on a program (the Close-Holton experiment) in which the effects of behavior modification and transactional analysis were compared. The study was carried out in two institutions, each housing 400 youths between ages 15 and 17 years, under the California Youth Authority. The study is one of the few that gave estimates of how much each setting implemented the programs as originally outlined in the protocols. Outcome was assessed by using a number of instruments and follow-up reconviction rates for up to 2 years. Youths in both programs made academic progress beyond what was expected. Behavior modification was more effective in changing behavior of those who were termed *acting-out neurotics*. By 2 years, 47% of youths from each setting violated parole and had been returned to the institution. Positive regard, a measure of the staffs' impressions of a subject's relationship with the staff, was higher in the group that had more improvement and accounted for as much of a variance of outcome as did the two treatments. The two treatments were approximately equal, and both were better than no treatment.

In contrast to the institutional setting of the California Youth Authority program, Wolff et al. (1976) described a program (Achievement Place) featuring small group-home treatment and based on behavior modification principles. A trained child care couple lived in a home with six youths who had repeated contacts with juvenile authorities. Follow-up of the original group compared with the control group did not reveal significant differences in offense rates, although during the treatment phase the treatment group did better than the control group.

Strain et al. (1982) reported a 3- to 9-year follow-up of children ages 3–5 years who exhibited severe and prolonged tantrums, continual opposition to requests, and physical aggression toward parents. Both teachers and parents reported improvement, and the behavior of the former patients was similar to that of their peers. Only the age that treatment began and family intactness were related to current levels of behavior. These two variables, family intactness and age that treatment began, are repeated in the literature. The earlier treatment begins, the greater the chance of success.

Safer et al. (1981) reported a 4-year follow-up of a behavioral program for disruptive junior high school students. The program was a collaborative one between a community mental health center and the school. It was a comprehensive, behavioral, in-school, regular education project characterized by a token economy, parent contracting, major subjects taught in morning, small class enrollment, small group and individualized instruction, an early release contingency option, and frequent parent-school communications. Follow-up findings indicated that former students in the program had reduced suspensions, expulsions, and grade failure. In senior high school, they achieved a significantly higher entry rate, greater attendance, better classroom conduct, and a lower frequency of withdrawal from school.

Sanchez (1986) conducted a 25-year follow-up study of 165 men who were in a school for juvenile delinquents in 1950–1960. The study assessed the efficacy of milieu therapy. The antisocial subjects benefited most from the therapy regardless of treatment duration. With treatment lasting more than four years, almost 75% showed enduring benefit.

Shapiro and Sherman (1983) suggested that a child who becomes sociopathic in adolescence will be relatively unamenable to traditional psychiatric interventions designed for individual adolescents, although Garrett (1985) concluded that interventions such as contingency management, cognitive-behavior therapy, family therapy, and some of the life-skill observations warranted further research. Kazdin (1985) observed that techniques focusing on the problem-solving skills of the child and parents, child-rearing practices, and family interaction and family therapy have promise for treatment. Again, the younger the child is when treatment begins, the better the prognosis. Absence of marital discord and parental psychopathology was a significant protective factor against the development of conduct disorder in childhood and adolescence.

Although the literature on treatment of antisocial adolescents leads to negative conclusions for long-term effects (Kazdin 1987; J. Q. Wilson and Herrnstein 1985), there appears to be some optimism for successful treatment with children and preadolescents (Kazdin 1987; Patterson et al. 1989) when parent-training techniques, child social skills training, and academic remediation are used concurrently.

It is too late to help Carl, the youth discussed at the beginning of this chapter, but there may be hope for his children.

References

Behar D, Stewart MA: Aggressive conduct disorder in children. Acta Psychiatr Scand 65:210–220, 1982

Boyle MH, Offord DR: Primary prevention of conduct disorder: issues and prospects. J Am Acad Child Adolesc Psychiatry 29:227–233, 1990

Cadoret RJ: Psychopathology in adopted-away offspring of biological parents with antisocial behavior. Arch Gen Psychiatry 35:176–184, 1978

Cadoret RJ, Cain C, Crowe RR: Evidence for gene-environment interaction in the development of adolescent antisocial behavior. Behav Genet 13:301–310, 1983

Cass LA, Thomas CB: Childhood Pathology and Later Adjustment. New York, Wiley, 1979

Cloninger CR, Christiansen KO, Reich T, et al: Implications of sex differences in the prevalences of antisocial personality, alcoholism, and criminality for familial transmission. Arch Gen Psychiatry 35:941–951, 1978

Cloninger CR, Sigoardsson S, Bohman M: Predisposition to petty criminality in Swedish adoptees, II: cross-fostering analysis of gene-environment interaction. Arch Gen Psychiatry 39:1242, 1982

Faretra G: A profile of aggression from adolescence to adulthood: an 18 year follow-up of psychiatrically disturbed and violent adolescents. Am J Orthopsychiatry 51:439–453, 1981

Farrington DP: The family backgrounds of aggressive youths, in Aggression and Antisocial Behavior in Childhood and Adolescence. Edited by Hersov LA, Berger M, Shaffer D. Oxford, England, Pergamon, 1978

Garrett CJ: Effects of residential treatment on adjudicated delinquents: a meta-analysis. Journal of Research, Crime and Delinquency 22:287–308, 1985

Glueck S, Glueck E: Unraveling Juvenile Delinquency. Cambridge, MA, Harvard University Press, 1950

Glueck S, Glueck E: Predicting Delinquency and Crime. Cambridge, MA, Harvard University Press, 1959

Glueck S, Glueck E: Delinquents and Nondelinquents in Perspective. Cambridge, MA, Harvard University Press, 1968

Henn FA, Bardwell R, Jenkins RL: Juvenile delinquents revisited. Arch Gen Psychiatry 37:1160–1163, 1980

Hetherington EM, Martin B: Family interaction, in Psychopathological Disorders of Childhood, 2nd Edition. Edited by Quay HC, Werry JS. New York, Wiley, 1979, pp 30–82

Huesmann LR, Eron LD, Lofhourtz MM, et al: Stability of aggression over time and generations. Dev Psychol 20:1120–1134, 1984

Institute of Medicine: Research on Children and Adolescents With Mental, Behavior, and Developmental Disorders. Washington, DC, National Academy Press, 1989

Jesness CF: Comparative effectiveness of behavior modifications and transactional programs for delinquents. J Consult Clin Psychol 43:758–779, 1975

Kazdin AE: Treatment of Antisocial Behavior in Children and Adolescents. Homewood, IL, Dorsey Press, 1985

Kazdin AE: Conduct Disorders in Childhood and Adolescence. Beverly Hills, CA, Sage, 1986

Kazdin AE: Treatment of antisocial behavior in children: current status and future directions. Psychol Bull 102:187–203, 1987

Lewis DO, Shanok SS, Grant M, et al: Homicidally aggressive young children: neuropsychiatric and experimental correlates. Am J Psychiatry 140:148–153, 1983

Lipton D, Martinson R, Wilks J: The Effectiveness of Correctional Treatment: A Survey of Treatment Evaluation Studies. New York, Praeger, 1975

Locher R, Dishion TJ: Boys who fight at home and school: family conditions influencing cross-setting consistency. J Consult Clin Psychol 52:759–768, 1984

McCord JA: Thirty year follow-up of treatment effects. Am Psychol 33:284–289, 1978

McCord W, Sanchez J: The treatment of deviant children: a twenty-five year follow-up study. Crime and Delinquency 29:238–253, 1983

McCord W, McCord J, Zola LK: Origins of Crime: A New Evaluation of the Cambridge-Somerville Youth Study. New York, Columbia University Press, 1959

Mednick SA, Hutchings B: Genetic and psychophysiological factors in asocial behavior, in Psychopathic Behavior: Approaches to Research. Edited by Hare RD, Schalling D. Chichester, England, John Wiley, 1978

Mitchell S, Rosa P: Boyhood behavior problems as precursors of criminality: a fifteen-year follow-up study. J Child Psychol Psychiatry 22:19–33, 1981

Palmer T: The Youth Authority's Community Treatment Project. Federal Probation 38:3–14, 1974

Patterson GR, Debaryske BD, Ramsey E: A developmental perspective on antisocial behavior. Am Psychol 44:329–335, 1989

Quay HC: Conduct disorders, in Psychopathological Disorders of Childhood. Edited by Quay HC, Werry JS. New York, Wiley, 1986, pp 35–72

Quay HC (ed): Handbook of Juvenile Delinquency. New York, Wiley, 1987

Robins LN: Deviant Children Grown Up. Baltimore, MD, Williams & Wilkins, 1966

Robins LN: Sturdy childhood predictors of adult antisocial behavior: replications from longitudinal studies. Psychol Med 8:611–622, 1978

Robins LN: Sturdy childhood predictors of adult outcome replications from longitudinal studies, in Stress and Mental Disorder. Edited by Barrett JE, Rose RM, Klerman GL. New York, Raven, 1979, pp 219–235

Rutsma-Street M, Offord DR, Finch T: Pairs of same sexed siblings discordant for antisocial behavior. Br J Psychiatry 146:415–423, 1985

Rutter M, Giller H: Juvenile Delinquency: Trends and Perspectives. New York, Penguin, 1983

Rutter M, Manghan B, Mortinore P, et al: Fifteen Thousand Hours: Secondary Schools and Their Effects on Children. Cambridge, MA, Harvard University Press, 1979

Safer DJ, Heaton RC, Parker FC: A behavioral program for disruptive junior high school students: results and follow up. J Abnorm Child Psychol 9:483–494, 1981

Sanchez J: The use of milieu therapy in treating the antisocial personality. Residential Treatment for Children and Youth 4:25–38, 1986

Shapiro T, Sherman M: Long-term follow-up of children with psychiatric disorders. Hospital and Community Psychiatry 34:522–527, 1983

Strain PS, Steele P, Ellis T, et al: Long-term effects of oppositional child treatment with mothers as therapists and therapist trainers. J Appl Behav Anal 15:163–169, 1982

West DJ: Delinquency: Its Roots, Careers and Prospects. Cambridge, MA, Harvard University Press, 1982

Wilson H: Parental supervision: a neglected aspect of delinquency. British Journal of Criminology 20:203–235, 1980

Wilson JQ, Herrnstein RJ: Crime and Human Nature. New York, Simon & Schuster, 1985

Wodarski JS: Follow-up on behavioral intervention with troublesome adolescents. J Behav Ther Exp Psychiatry 10:181–188, 1979

Wolff MM, Philips EL, Fixsen DL, et al: Achievement Place: the teaching family model. Child Care Quarterly 5:92–103, 1976

11

Outcome of Childhood Pathology: Single Versus Comorbid Disorders

Almost all of the children described in the vignettes that begin most of the previous chapters had more than one psychiatric problem (i.e., had comorbid conditions). This chapter, on effects of comorbid disorders in childhood, can be read with their stories in mind.

Comorbidity, the simultaneous occurrence of two or more childhood psychopathological conditions, is a perplexing and interesting problem in child psychiatry. From a developmental perspective, comorbid disorders may reflect amorphous, nonspecific expressions of symptom patterns in younger children, in contrast to clearer clinical presentations in older children or adolescents. Such "boundary" problems between disorders may be due to nonspecific early responses to family psychopathology (Carlson 1990). Similarly, it has been suggested that co-occurring disorders in children and adolescents may result from shared risk factors or overlap between risk factors—for example, in comorbid depression and conduct disorder, depressed parents for the former and family disorder for the latter (Rutter 1989). Comorbidity simply may be the changing expression of a disorder with age or developmental stage; thus, the apparent development of a new disorder may reflect the developmental progression of the same underlying pathological process. Also, psychopathology may interfere with the developmentally appropriate acquisition of social and academic skills, which become increasingly important for daily functioning in later childhood and adolescence. As a result, a comorbid second or third disorder may develop because early problems remain unresolved (Caron and Rutter 1991).

In this chapter, data from cross-sectional and longitudinal studies of child and adolescent psychopathology are examined to determine the extent to which existing data illuminate questions of etiology, the developmental progression from one disorder to another is mapped, and factors influencing the course and outcome of disorders alone or in combination are revealed. Other chapters in this volume have drawn more heavily on clinical samples; this chapter has drawn principally on epidemiological studies. Epidemiological studies hold great promise to clarify the nature of risk and protective factors that mediate the course and outcome of single and comorbid forms of disorder, apart from factors related to treatment seeking or referral (e.g., severity, comorbidity). Also, whereas the other chapters in this volume focus more on the outcome of specific disorders, this chapter compares and contrasts the outcomes of single and comorbid presentations of disorder.

Prevalence of Psychopathology: Age and Sex Differences

Some evidence concerning continuities and discontinuities of single and comorbid forms of psychopathology can be found in recent prevalence studies of child and adolescent psychopathology. During the past decade, there has been a remarkable increase in the available data on child and adolescent disorders based on general population studies. Gould et al. (1981) reviewed 25 studies (published 1928 through 1974) and estimated the prevalence of childhood disorders to be 11.8%. Reviews of epidemiological studies by Brandenburg et al. (1990), Costello (1990), Fleming et al. (1989), and Offord et al. (1987) have indicated that the prevalence of child and adolescent mental disorders based on DSM-III (American Psychiatric Association 1980) criteria ranges from 5% to 26%. The larger, more methodologically rigorous general population studies suggest prevalence rates in a narrower range (17.6%–22%). Most of the studies show, in childhood, a higher prevalence rate of disorders for boys than for girls, but in adolescence the rate is higher for girls than for boys. Many of these gender-related differences are disorder and age specific (Table 11–1).

For instance, rates of conduct disorder tend to be higher in adoles-

Table 11–1.   Examples of rates of disorder by age and gender

	Conduct disorder	Oppositional defiant disorder	Attention-deficit/ hyperactivity disorder	Anxiety
Peaks in	Mid-adolescence	Adolescence	Late childhood/ early adolescence	Variable by category
Gender	Higher for boys	Similar	Higher for boys	Higher for girls

cence than in childhood, peaking in mid-adolescence. Consistently, rates are substantially higher for boys than for girls (Anderson et al. 1987; Bird et al. 1988; McGee et al. 1992b; Offord et al. 1987; Velez et al. 1989). Recent data from the New York Child Longitudinal Study (Cohen et al. 1993) suggest that the prevalence rate of conduct disorder decreases in late adolescence. Rates for oppositional defiant disorder also tend to be higher in adolescence than in childhood but, unlike rates for conduct disorder, are quite similar for boys and girls (Anderson et al. 1987; Bird et al. 1988; Cohen et al. 1993; Feehan et al. 1993; McGee et al. 1992b; Velez et al. 1989). In contrast, rates for attention-deficit disorder generally have been found to be higher for boys than for girls and tend to peak in late childhood and early adolescence.

In the instance of the more commonly occurring anxiety disorders and the overarching diagnostic category of anxiety disorders, the prevalence rates tend to be high, especially for girls (Feehan et al. 1993; Kashani et al. 1987, 1989). For specific conditions, such as separation anxiety disorder, the rate tends to be highest in late childhood (Velez et al. 1989) and quite low in adolescence. Whether separation anxiety disorder may be a forerunner of other anxiety disorders (e.g., overanxious disorder, which is more prevalent in adolescence) is an interesting unanswered question. For overanxious disorder, in contrast, there is some evidence that the rate is relatively low during childhood (Costello et al. 1988) but rises during early adolescence (Velez et al. 1989). Data from the New York Child Longitudinal Study sample (Cohen et al. 1993) suggest that the increased cases in adolescence are contributed to primarily by girls.

Depressive disorder rates were quite variable across studies, ranging from a low of 1.4% in a New Zealand sample (Anderson et al. 1987) to the highest figures reported in the Ontario Child Health Study sample (13.6%) (Offord et al. 1987). Rates for depressive disorders tend to be more similar for boys and girls in childhood than in adolescence; in adolescence, they generally were higher for girls than for boys (e.g., Cohen et al. 1993).

From a developmental perspective, questions must be raised concerning the antecedents, correlates, and sequelae of these disorders and the extent to which these factors are sex related. For attention-deficit disorder, it is possible that sex-related predispositions and biological substrates of the disorder may account for higher rates in boys than for girls. For both affective and anxiety disorders, there are higher rates for girls than for boys. It is unclear to what extent various psychosocial and biological factors may contribute to the emergence of gender differences in early to mid-adolescence. Possibly age- and sex-related patterns found in diagnostic prevalence studies are a function of the particular taxonomy embedded in DSM descriptive language. However, similar patterns have been reported in studies using non-DSM dimensional approaches. For example, Achenbach et al. (1991) conducted a national survey of problems and competencies among children ages 4–16 years, collecting data on 2,600 referred and 2,600 matched nonreferred children. They found a decline with age for total behavior problems in the nonreferred sample (but an opposite tendency in the referred sample). They also found that externalizing problems decreased, whereas internalizing problems increased with age. In general, their findings supported the sex difference findings from the general population studies described previously, in that boys tended to score higher on externalizing problems and syndromes, whereas girls tended to score higher on internalizing problems and syndromes.

Continuities and Discontinuities

Consider the stability and continuity of disorders diagnosed in childhood. Data are available on continuities and discontinuities in child and adolescent disorders. Some derive from general population studies that focus on categorical classification of disorders (diagnoses based on DSM and *International Classification of Diseases* [ICD] criteria), and some derive from studies focusing on emotional symptoms or behavior problems. McGee et al. (1992b) examined the longitudinal course of disorders in 750 children seen at age 11 years and at age 15 years as part of the Dunedin, New Zealand, study (McGee and Williams 1988). (See also Chapters 4 and 7 in this volume.) At each time of assessment, they inquired about the preceding 12 months. Of the 66 children who had a disorder at age 11 years, only 42% had a disorder at age 15 years. Of the 147 children with diagnoses at age 15 years, the majority (81%) had been diagnosis free at age 11 years. Regardless of diagnoses at age 11 years, 4 years later, at age 15, boys were more likely to have externalizing disorders and girls were more likely to have internalizing disorders.

In later reports from the same study, Feehan et al. (1993) followed the longitudinal course of disorders in 890 adolescents of the Dunedin sample seen at age 15 years and again 3 years later at age 18 years, also focusing on the 12 months preceding the interview. Of the adolescents with diagnosed conditions at age 15 years ($n = 191$), 63% also had a disorder at age 18 years. Of the 323 adolescents with diagnoses at age 18 years, the majority (62.5%) were diagnosis free at age 15 years. Whereas externalizing disorders at age 15 years were associated with both internalizing and externalizing disorders at age 18 years, internalizing disorders at age 15 years were more likely to be associated with internalizing than with externalizing disorders at age 18 years.

In further analyses, Feehan et al. (1993) used anxiety, depression, substance use, and conduct disorder symptom scores to explore differences among adolescents with transient (age 15 years only), recurrent (ages 15 and 18 years), and new (age 18 years) disorders. For adolescents age 15 years, the combined scores for the four symptom scales were significantly higher in the recurrent than in the transient group, and the new disorder group had elevated symptom scores compared with the no-diagnosis group. For adolescents age 18 years, the recurrent disorder group had significantly higher total symptom scores than those of the new disorder group. Moreover, the adolescents in the recurrent group were more likely than adolescents in the new disorder group to have an externalizing disorder as well as three or more disorders.

In an epidemiological study in Mannheim, Germany, Esser et al. (1990) reported that of 71 children with diagnoses at age 8 years, only 51% continued to have a disorder at age 13 years. In addition, of 78 children with diagnoses at age 13 years, 54% had been disorder free at age 8 years. The best predictors among several child and family attributes of psychiatric disorder in children at age 13 years were psychiatric disorder, specific learning disabilities, and family adversity at age 8 years as well as a number of life events when children were between ages 8 and 13 years. Two significant indicators of remission (disorder at age 8 years, no disorder at age 13 years) were absence of conduct disorder at age 8 years and improvement of adverse family conditions.

It is instructive to consider cross-age comparisons of disorders if disorders are grouped into three categories: 1) internalizing or neurotic (neurotic and emotional disorders plus emotional problems with conduct symptoms), 2) externalizing or disruptive behavior disorders and conduct disorders, and 3) developmentally related disorders (attention-deficit/hyperkinetic syndromes plus specific child psychiatric syndromes such as autistic disorder). So examined, the data show that children with neurotic disorders had the best prognosis; children with conduct disorder had the worst prognosis. Thus, of the children with neurotic diagnoses at age 8 years, about 75% were diagnosis free at age 13 years. In contrast, of the children with conduct disorders at age 8 years, most still had conduct disorders at age 13 years. Of the children with developmentally related disorders at age eight years, about half were diagnosis free at age 13 years.

Verhulst and Althaus (1988) reported on persistence and change in behavioral/emotional problems, based on parent report of children ages 4–11 years over a 2-year period ($N = 1,412$). Of children ages 4–5 years, 6–11 years, and 12–14 years with scores in the deviant range (above the 90th percentile) at initial assessment, a large percentage (46%, 55%, and 56%, respectively) continued to score in the deviant range 2 years later. Verhulst and van der Ende (1993) examined predictive relations of syndromes in the same children ages 4–11 years across a 6-year period. Based on quantitative scores, the highest correlations generally were between the same syndromes across time—that is, for aggressive behavior ($r = .58$), attention problems ($r = .47$), withdrawn behavior ($r = .46$), anxious/depressed behavior ($r = .45$), delinquent behavior ($r = .37$), and social problems ($r = .36$). Based on categorical scores (deviant versus nondeviant), odds ratios of the degree to which deviance in each of the syndromes predicted deviance in the same as well as the other syndromes 6 years later yielded similar results. In general, the highest odds ratios were found for deviance in the same syndrome and within each of the broadband syndromes (internalizing and externalizing problems).

Summary

From general population studies comes evidence of less continuity in psychiatric disorders from childhood to early adolescence (e.g., Esser et al. 1990) or from early to mid-adolescence (e.g., McGee et al. 1992b) than from mid- to late adolescence (e.g., Feehan et al. 1993). In general, studies indicate that of children and adolescents with disorders at a particular time, more than half previously had been diagnosis free.

From studies of particular disorders we learn the following: children with externalizing disorders are more likely than children with internalizing disorders to have a diagnosable condition at follow-up. It is noteworthy that the majority of those who have internalizing disorders in early adolescence are diagnosis free when assessed in childhood (e.g., Esser et al. 1990). Adolescents with externalizing disorders earlier in adolescence are almost equally likely to have internalizing or externalizing disorders in later adolescence, whereas those with internalizing disorders earlier in adolescence are more likely to continue to have internalizing disorders than to develop externalizing disorders (Feehan et al. 1993). Those with recurrent disorders are more likely to have multiple disorders than those who previously had been diagnosis free. Among adolescents, there is some evidence of greater continuity for externalizing disorders for boys and for internalizing disorders for girls. Moreover, boys with either internalizing or externalizing disorders are more likely to have externalizing than internalizing disorders at follow-up (e.g., McGee et al. 1992b).

Single Versus Comorbid Disorders: Predictors, Course, and Outcome

Longitudinal studies focusing on the course and predictors of comorbid disorders in nonreferred samples are few. Therefore, community- and school-based studies that report on behavior problems, as well as those that report on psychiatric disorders, are reviewed.

In the Ontario Child Health Study, Fleming et al. (1993) studied the longitudinal course of conduct disorder and major depressive symptoms in 650 adolescents (333 boys and 317 girls), ages 13–16 years, who were followed up 4 years later when they were ages 17–20 years. The investigators compared four diagnostic groups: 1) those with major depressive symptoms, 2) those with conduct disorder, 3) those with both major depressive symptoms and conduct disorder, and 4) healthy control subjects (Table 11–2).

Moffitt (1990) examined the developmental trajectories of 435 boys in the Dunedin sample identified for study by their self-reported delin-

Table 11–2. Longitudinal course of comorbidity over 4 years

Original diagnosis	Major depressive symptoms	Conduct disorder	Major depressive symptoms + conduct disorder	Control subjects
Comorbid major depressive disorder	25.0%	16.7%	11.1%	6.9%
Comorbid dysthymia	16.0%	16.7%	7.7%	4.1%
Comorbid generalized anxiety disorder	28.6%	14.8%	24.1%	15.1%
Comorbid drug abuse/ dependence	3.6%	23.1%	28.6%	2.1%
Comorbid alcohol abuse/ dependence	24.1%	17.9%	57.1%	14.8%

Source. Fleming et al. 1993.

quent behavior and clinical diagnosis of attention-deficit disorder at age 13 years (Table 11–3). Four groups were formed: 1) those with attention-deficit disorder and delinquency, 2) those with attention-deficit disorder only, 3) those with delinquency only, and 4) healthy control subjects.

Available data at ages 3, 5, 7, 9, 11, and 13 years on antisocial behavior, family adversity, verbal cognitive ability, and reading achievement were compared in these four groups. At all ages, boys in the attention-deficit disorder plus delinquency group consistently had higher levels of antisocial behavior, greater family adversity, poorer verbal ability, and lower levels of reading achievement than did the boys in the three other groups. In relation to the other groups, the children in the attention-deficit disorder plus delinquency group also showed motor skills deficits early in life and verbal IQ deficits by age 5 years. The greatest increase in antisocial behavior in the attention-deficit disorder plus delinquency group occurred between ages 5 and 7 years, coinciding with relatively low reading achievement following school entry. At that early age, those in the attention-deficit disorder plus delinquency group had a level of antisocial behavior that was not in evidence in the delinquency only group until age 13 years. The delinquency only group had trajectories similar to those of the attention-deficit disorder only group and control group until age 13 years, when the level of their antisocial behavior, which defined them as delinquent, approached that of the attention-deficit disorder plus delinquency group.

Anderson et al. (1989) compared cognitive and social correlates for children at ages 5, 7, 9, and 11 years who had DSM-III disorders diagnosed at age 11 years in the Dunedin sample ($N = 798$). The following groups were examined: those with anxiety/depression ($n = 23$), those with attention-deficit disorder ($n = 36$), those with conduct disorder/oppositional defiant disorder ($n = 21$), those with multiple disor-

Table 11–3. Attention-deficit disorder and delinquency

	Attention deficit disorder + delinquency	Attention deficit disorder	Delinquency only
Birth cohort	4%	4%	12%
Cases	50%	46%	73%

Source. Moffitt 1990.

ders (n = 16), and control subjects with no disorders (n = 702). For cognitive measures (verbal IQ, full-scale IQ, reading, and spelling), children in the attention-deficit disorder and multiple disorders groups had significantly lower scores than did children in the other groups. These findings held across time when controlled for sex and cumulative family disadvantage differences. Only children in the multiple disorders group were increasingly more disliked and solitary across age, based on a peer socialization measure. However, children in the attention-deficit disorder and multiple disorders groups generally had lower self-esteem scores than those of the sample mean. Finally, with few changes across time, family adversity was highest for the multiple disorders group, followed by the conduct disorder/oppositional defiant disorder, attention-deficit disorder, anxiety/depression, and control groups.

McGee et al. (1992a) examined the course of attention-deficit disorder in 45 children (40 boys, 5 girls) diagnosed at age 11 years, with onset at three different ages: 3 years (n = 15), 5–6 years (n = 15), and 7 years (n = 15). The investigators compared these children with 369 children who were without diagnoses (Table 11–4). The diagnoses of children described as having attention-deficit disorder at age 11 years were based on parent, teacher, and self-identification in the two earliest-onset groups (ages 3 years and 5–6 years) and on teacher and self-identification in the later-onset group (age 7 years). Almost all of the disorders comorbid with attention-deficit disorder in children age 11 years were conduct disorder/oppositional defiant disorder or conduct disorder/oppositional defiant disorder plus anxiety/depression.

Frost et al. (1989) investigated neuropsychological deficits in a sample of children age 13 years in the Dunedin sample (N = 678), comparing children with diagnoses of attention-deficit disorder (n = 13), conduct disorder (n = 17), anxiety (n = 14), depression (n = 10), and multiple disorders (n = 19) versus those with no disorders (n = 605).

Table 11–4. Comorbidity course of attention-deficit disorder

Age of onset	Comorbid by age 11	Comorbid by age 15
Age 3	67%	67%
Ages 5–6	61%	77%
Age 7	27%	31%

Source.   McGee et al. 1992a.

The investigators used "strict and multiple diagnostic criteria" (Table 11–5).

Verhulst and van der Ende (1993) examined the course of attention, conduct, and anxiety/depression problems in the deviant range (cross-informant syndromes on the Child Behavior Checklist [CBCL; Achenbach 1987], based on parent report), including comorbid problems, over a 6-year period in children ages 4–11 years. Focusing on attention and conduct problems, the investigators compared children who were deviant at initial assessment in both syndromes ($n = 76$) with children who were deviant only in attention problems ($n = 35$) or only in conduct problems ($n = 12$). They found that children with "mixed" problems had the worst outcome 6 years later. Similarly, focusing on anxiety/depression and conduct problems, they compared children who initially were deviant in both syndromes ($n = 62$) with children who were deviant only in anxiety/depression problems ($n = 40$) or only in conduct problems ($n = 14$). Again, those with mixed problems had the worst outcome 6 years later. Finally, focusing on attention and anxiety/depression problems, the investigators compared children deviant in both syndromes ($n = 56$) with children deviant only in attention ($n = 13$) or only in anxiety/depression problems ($n = 27$). The mixed group had the worst outcome 6 years later. In addition, Verhulst and van der Ende (1993) compared children who initially were deviant in both internalizing and externalizing behaviors ($n = 56$) with children who were deviant in only one of these syndromes (internalizing, $n = 15$; externalizing, $n = 27$) and in the normal range on the other. At the broadband level, the children in the mixed category also had the worst outcome.

Another study of the course of comorbid behavior problems was conducted by Capaldi (1992), who examined elevated conduct problems (above the 70th percentile on the Teacher Version of the CBCL [Achenbach 1982]), elevated depression symptoms, and co-occurrence of elevated conduct problems and elevated depression symptoms in a

Table 11–5. Frequency of generalized neuropsychological deficits

Multiple disorders	Attention deficit disorder	Anxiety	Conduct disorder	Depression
26.3%	15.4%	71.%	0%	0%

Source. Frost et al. 1989.

community sample of sixth-grade boys who attended schools in a high-crime area. They were followed up after 2 years, when they were in eighth grade (N = 201). Assessment of conduct problems was based on teacher ratings on the CBCL; assessment of depression symptoms was based on boys' self-report on the Children's Depression Rating Scale (CDRS; Poznanski 1979). Across the 2-year period, stability of conduct problems was greater (r = .78) than stability of depression symptoms (r = .40). Moreover, among boys in the early-onset conduct problems group, there was a significant increase in depression symptoms, but there was no significant increase in conduct problems among boys in the early-onset depression symptoms group.

Of the 35 boys initially in the conduct problems group, 42% were in the same group 2 years later, 22% changed to the conduct problems plus depression symptoms group, 8% changed to the depression symptoms group, and 25% no longer had conduct problems. Of the 30 boys initially in the depression symptoms group, 36% did not change, 10% changed to the conduct problems group, 3% changed to the conduct problems plus depression symptoms group, and almost half (48%) no longer had depression symptoms. Of the 23 boys initially in the conduct problems plus depression symptoms group, 48% were in the same group 2 years later, 26% changed to the conduct problems group, 17% changed to the depression symptoms group, and only 9% no longer had symptoms. Thus, the boys in the conduct problems plus depression symptoms group had the worst outcome, whereas those in the depression symptoms group had the best outcome.

In an 18-year follow-up study of child and adolescent depression, Harrington et al. (1991) found different outcomes between those with initial diagnoses of depression and those with initial diagnoses of depression comorbid with conduct disorder (n = 63). The investigators examined whether depression comorbid with conduct disorder is different from depression alone and whether depression is secondary to conduct disorder. Of the 63 depression patients, 46% had one conduct disorder symptom (DSM-III-R [American Psychiatric Association 1987] criteria) and 21% had three or more other symptoms. Of the psychiatric control subjects (n = 68), 25% had three or more other symptoms. At the 18-year follow-up, the Lifetime Version of the Schedule for Affective Disorders and Schizophrenia (Spitzer and Endicott 1975) was administered (Research Diagnostic Criteria [RDC]). In the short term, those with depression plus conduct disorder improved less and appeared more handicapped than those with depression alone; in adulthood, those with depression plus conduct disorder were more likely than those with depression alone, as well as healthy control subjects, to have antisocial personality disorder and were more likely than those with depression alone to be at risk for alcohol abuse and dependence. In addition, trends indicated that those with depression only were at greater risk for a major depressive disorder in adulthood than those with depression plus conduct disorder but that those with depression plus conduct disorder were more impaired than those with depression only. It appears that depression plus conduct disorder has different implications than depression only so that adolescents with depression plus conduct disorder have a course consistent with conduct disorder, whereas those with depression only have a course relatively more consistent with "pure" depressive disorders in adulthood.

Temporal Ordering of Comorbidity

Relatively little is known about the temporal order of comorbid conditions. Rohde et al. (1991) reported on the temporal order of comorbid depression in their community sample of adolescents ages 14–18 years ($N = 1,710$). Based on current and lifetime comorbidity of depression, they found that, with the exception of eating disorders, there was a significantly greater likelihood for comorbid disorders to follow than to precede depression (79.1% versus 20.9%, respectively). This likelihood also applied to substance abuse (64.5% versus 35.5%), disruptive behavior (71.8% versus 28.2%), and especially anxiety (85.1% versus 14.9%). In the same sample, Lewinsohn et al. (1991) examined the temporal order of comorbid depressive disorders, major depressive disorder, and dysthymic disorder and found that of 292 adolescents with a lifetime diagnosis of major depressive disorder, 43 (14.7%) had had two episodes (both major depressive disorder). None of the adolescents with a lifetime diagnosis of dysthymic disorder had had more than one episode. For 21 of the 23 (91.3%) adolescents who had a lifetime diagnosis of major depressive disorder and dysthymic disorder, the episode of dysthymic disorder preceded the episode of major depressive disorder, a temporal sequence that did not differ for males and females. These findings suggest that it is highly likely that a dysthymic episode in adolescence will be followed by an episode of major depression.

Kovacs et al. (1989) reported on comorbid anxiety disorders in a sample of 104 of 143 depressed children, who had come into the study during its first 6 years when the mean follow-up interval was 3 years. Of those children, 43 (41.3%) had depression comorbid with anxiety disorders at the outset, 32 had comorbid separation anxiety, and 17 had comorbid overanxious disorder. Another three children developed anxiety disorders over the observation period. The age-corrected cumulative risk to age 18 years for anxiety disorder in childhood-onset depression was .47, with anxiety most likely to manifest before a child was age 12 years. However, the presence of anxiety did not appear to influence the risk for subsequent depressive episodes. The children with comorbid anxiety disorders were younger than the other children in the sample. Among the children who had comorbid major depressive disorder and anxiety, anxiety preceded major depressive disorder two-thirds of the time; in one-third of these children, the onset of anxiety was either at the same time as major depressive disorder or followed the onset of major depressive disorder. Comorbid anxiety was equally likely to persist and not persist after major depressive disorder had remitted. Temporal order findings were different for the small number of children who had dysthymic disorder comorbid with anxiety ($n = 9$). In only two of the nine patients did anxiety precede the onset of dysthymic disorder. Thus, the temporal order findings for dysthymic disorder comorbid with anxiety, but not for major depressive disorder comorbid with anxiety, are similar to the findings in lifetime diagnoses by Rohde et al. (1991) that comorbid disorders appear more likely to follow than to precede depressive disorders.

Kovacs et al. (1988) reported on comorbid conduct disorder in the same 104 children when the mean follow-up interval was 3 years. They found that 17 of the children (16.3%) had comorbid conduct disorder at the outset and that another 7 children developed conduct disorder after their index episode of depression remitted (23% total). Five of the 17 depressed children who had comorbid conduct disorder had several episodes of conduct disorder, and 3 of these 5 children eventually developed bipolar disorder. Two of the seven children who developed conduct disorder later also eventually developed bipolar disorder. There were no sex differences for depression with or without conduct disorder. However, the presence of attention-deficit disorder in depressed girls, but not in boys, appeared to shorten the time to onset of conduct disorder. Older age at onset of depression was associated with the presence of comorbid conduct disorder, and conduct disorder was most likely to manifest at ages 11–14 years. The age-corrected cumulative risk to age 19 years for conduct disorder in childhood-onset depression was .36. Among the children who had major depressive disorder or dysthymic disorder comorbid with conduct disorder, conduct disorder was most likely to follow the onset of depression. Comorbid conduct disorder was likely to persist after depression remitted. Thus, the findings for depressive disorders comorbid with conduct disorder in the Kovacs et al. (1988) study were similar to those in the study by Rohde et al. (1991).

Summary

In general, children and adolescents with multiple disorders are more likely to have continuing problems than those with a single diagnosis. There is evidence that children with comorbid disruptive disorders tend to have an early onset of problem behavior and difficulties with social and academic functioning that persist into adolescence (e.g., Anderson et al. 1989; Fergusson et al. 1993; Frost et al. 1989; McGee et al. 1992a; Moffitt 1990). Children with emotional disorders or problems that are comorbid with disruptive disorders also appear to fare worse than children with only one of these disorders or problems (e.g., Fleming et al. 1993; Verhulst and van der Ende 1993). Among adolescents with diagnoses of major depressive symptoms comorbid with conduct disorder at ages 13–16 years, for instance, there was a higher rate at follow-up 4 years later of alcohol and drug abuse and dependence than among adolescents with major depressive symptoms only and a higher rate of major depressive symptoms, dysthymic disorder, generalized anxiety disorder, and alcohol abuse and dependence than among adolescents with conduct disorder only (Fleming et al. 1993). Similarly, among sixth-grade boys, those with both conduct problems and depressive symptoms were more likely to continue to have problems in eighth grade (91%) than were boys with conduct problems only (75%) or boys with depressive symptoms only (52%) (Capaldi 1992). Verhulst and van der Ende (1993) consistently found more children scoring in the deviant range in two syndromes than in only one of the syndromes. Initial behavior problems predicted not only similar but also different problem behavior 6 years later. Their findings led them to suggest that comorbidity may reflect the actual complexity of child psychopathology.

Conclusions

A basic finding in developmental studies of child and adolescent psychopathology is that boys and girls differ in how psychopathology is expressed and these differences tend to become more pronounced over time. Thus, depression may be twice as common in girls as in boys, especially after puberty, whereas attention-deficit/hyperactivity disorder may be more common in boys than in girls, regardless of age. Basic patterns of prevalence show these differences, but it is less clear if patterns of comorbidity also differ in boys and girls. For example, beyond simple prevalence questions, once there is evidence of depression, is it more (or less) likely in boys or girls to be comorbid with other conditions (e.g., conduct disorder, oppositional defiant disorder, attention-deficit/hyperactivity disorder, or anxiety disorder)? Only Bird et al. (1993) have begun to address such questions by examining age and sex differences in observed versus expected comorbidity among more than two disorders (i.e., attention-deficit disorder, conduct disorder/oppositional defiant disorder, anxiety, and depression). They found only one significant age difference for attention-deficit disorder plus depression (a higher than expected observed rate among children ages 9–12 years than among adolescents ages 13–16 years) and no significant sex differences. The general lack of such data, especially in longitudinal form, is not surprising. Large samples would have to be followed over time so that permutations in various comorbid subgroups can be examined by gender and age. In fact, such an effort may require aggregation across studies that use uniform methods of assessment and diagnosis.

Longitudinal research is needed to address many developmental questions. Children and adolescents must be studied repeatedly to examine developmental pathways and temporal ordering of various forms of psychopathology and to explore the possibility that one condition may be the early manifestation of a later form of psychopathology. A good example of the type of research needed is the work that Loeber et al. (1993) have done on oppositional defiant disorder and conduct disorder, which suggests that oppositional defiant disorder is an early manifestation of conduct disorder. A closely related consideration is that one disorder may precede or lead to another. Other examples of this type of research are the work of Kovacs et al. (1988, 1989) on depression and McGee et al. (1992a) on attention-deficit disorder.

This review of longitudinal studies suggests that what we call *comorbidity* may be a categorical description of the complex nature of the developing human organism. The less-differentiated expression of psychopathology in young children becomes more clearly defined as their personality begins to crystallize and their central nervous system approaches maturity, especially after puberty and mid-adolescence. The Rohde et al. (1991) study, for example, found comorbid disorders to be significantly lower in depressed adults than in depressed adolescents ages 14–18 years (42% in currently depressed adolescents and 43% in adolescents with a lifetime diagnosis of depression, with comparable current and lifetime rates in adults of 7.7% and 25.4%, respectively), suggesting that the finding of comorbidity may indeed be related to developmental phenomena.

Validity of various taxonomic approaches has been debated. The dichotomy between categorical (seeking to describe discrete syndromes, as in DSM) and dimensional (seeing symptoms as existing on a continuum) is characteristic of this debate. Edelbrock and Costello (1988) have suggested that a combination of categorical and dimensional approaches should be useful in the assessment of child psychopathology. Beyond problems with the validity of taxons, however, the various current descriptive approaches provide an opportunity to examine the phenomenology of emotional and behavioral problems. Given the complexity of the task, it would be prudent to try systematically to link the existing assessment approaches in order to determine which descriptors best apply under which conditions. Gould et al. (1993), taking the same approach as did Edelbrock and Costello (1988) with a referred sample, examined the convergence between CBCL syndromes and DSM-III diagnoses in a general population sample and came to similar conclusions (i.e., that it is informative to use dimensional as well as categorical assessment strategies). Their finding of direct linear relationships between corresponding CBCL scale scores and the percentage of children with DSM-III diagnoses, for example, makes it clear that such a dual approach should be especially useful in the investigation of comorbid disorders. Referring to the Puerto Rico study by Bird et al. (1992), Gould et al. (1993) stated, "Given the magnitude of comorbidity in the present community sample it would be a daunting and tedious task to define a sufficient set of combination categories to represent the extensive co-occurrence of disorders" (pp. 310–311).

If comorbidity reflects severity of psychopathology, then children with comorbid disorders would be seen more frequently at mental health and social services facilities than children with noncomorbid disorders. Indeed, data confirm this theory. In the Puerto Rico Psychiatry Epidemiologic Study, Bird et al. (1993) reported that, among children and adolescents with one diagnosis, 23% were receiving services, whereas, among those with two or more diagnoses, 77% were receiving services. The Dunedin Multidisciplinary Health and Development Study also showed that children age 13 years with multiple diagnoses (25%) were significantly more impaired than children with a single diagnosis (Frost et al. 1989).

It is clear that comorbidity must be considered in the design of research on disorders in children and adolescents—especially in the selection of psychiatric control groups—as well as in clinical practice. Brown and Barlow (1992) suggested that the following three questions need to be addressed in treatment research: 1) does the presence of certain comorbid disorders or symptoms affect the short- and long-term response to treatment? 2) what type of adjustments should and can be made to extant treatments to enhance treatment efficacy when comorbidity is present? and 3) what is the course of comorbid disorders and symptoms after successful treatment of the principal disorder? Comorbidity is likely to have implications for the evaluation of treatment efficacy.

As Kendall and Clarkin (1992) have noted, the study of comorbidity is "the premier challenge facing mental health professionals in the 1990s" (p. 833). Studies of the frequency of comorbidity and related conditions are greatly needed to include examination of symptom overlap and its potential role in defining boundaries between related disorders in addition to studies of different effects of treatment on children with comorbid disorders and on children who have the same disorder but different etiological factors.

Such studies may best be accomplished within the context of longitudinal epidemiological research with broad, developmentally appropriate measures of adaptations, strengths, and risk and protective factors across domains as well as measures of psychopathology. In this type of research, examining how children move into and out of areas of risk, dysfunction, and comorbidity is critical. If such research is to be fully successful, it must draw on both categorical and dimensional approaches to assessment. For maximum benefit to the mental health field, research must go beyond establishing base rates of child and adolescent disorders, must address taxonomic problems that exist in current child psychopathology research, and must determine how individual children change over their course of development. Although it is extraordinarily difficult and expensive to conduct longitudinal studies, the planned nationwide longitudinal epidemiological study of child and adolescent psychopathology in the United States could begin to address many pressing questions. Research problems posed by comorbidity are daunting, and much of the research in child psychopathology over the last decade has not addressed this issue satisfactorily. To the extent that children with comorbid disorders have been excluded from studies, past results may not be generalizable to children with comorbid conditions (usually the majority of children) who are seen in mental health settings. In addition, to the extent that children with comorbid disorders have been included in studies but their comorbidity characteristics have not been fully described, findings from studies may not be fully applicable to the presumed primary disorder. Such difficulties may explain discrepant or contradictory findings across studies.

The issue of comorbidity is not just one of methodological subtlety. It reaches to the heart of how we conceptualize child psychopathology. Through vigorous attempts to address these issues, by investigators from all relevant disciplines (clinical, epidemiological, developmental) who study children, we can hope to see quantitative and qualitative improvements in our conceptual approaches to child psychopathology over the next decade. Only by avoiding the reification of any of our current taxonomic and assessment approaches and by systematically building in "crosswalks" between the various alternatives in rigorous studies may we avoid rediscovering that comorbidity is the premier challenge facing mental health professionals in the year 2000 and beyond.

References

Achenbach TM, Edelbrock C: Manual for Child Behavioral Checklist and Revised Child Behavior Profile. Burlington, VT, University of Vermont, 1982

Achenbach TM, Howell CT, Quay HC, et al: National survey of problems and competencies among four- to sixteen-year-olds. Monogr Soc Res Child Dev 56 (series no 225):1–131, 1991

American Psychiatric Association: Diagnostic and Statistical Manual of Mental Disorders, 3rd Edition. Washington, DC, American Psychiatric Association, 1980

American Psychiatric Association: Diagnostic and Statistical Manual of Mental Disorders, 3rd Edition, Revised. Washington, DC, American Psychiatric Association, 1987

Anderson JC, Williams S, McGee R, et al: DSM-III disorders in preadolescent children: prevalence in a large sample from the general population. Arch Gen Psychiatry 44:69–76, 1987

Anderson JC, Williams S, McGee R, et al: Cognitive and social correlates of DSM-III disorders in preadolescent children. J Am Acad Child Adolesc Psychiatry 28:842–846, 1989

Bird H R, Canino G, Rubio-Stipec M, et al: Estimates of the prevalence of childhood maladjustment in a community survey in Puerto Rico. Arch Gen Psychiatry 45:1120–1126, 1988

Bird HR, Gould MS, Staghezza BM: Aggregating data from multiple informants in child psychiatry epidemiological research. J Am Acad Child Adolesc Psychiatry 31:78–85, 1992

Bird HR, Gould MS, Staghezza BM: Patterns of diagnostic comorbidity in a community sample of children aged 9 through 16 years. J Am Acad Child Adolesc Psychiatry 32:361–368, 1993

Brandenburg NA, Friedman RM, Silver SE: The epidemiology of childhood psychiatric disorders: prevalence findings from recent studies. J Am Acad Child Adolesc Psychiatry 29:76–83, 1990

Brown TA, Barlow DH: Comorbidity among anxiety disorders: implications for treatment and DSM-IV. J Consult Clin Psychol 60:835–844, 1992

Capaldi DM: Co-occurrence of conduct problems and depressive symptoms in early adolescent boys, II: a 2-year follow-up at grade 8. Dev Psychopathol 4: 125–144, 1992

Carlson GA: Annotation: child and adolescent mania: diagnostic considerations. J Child Psychol Psychiatry 31:331–341, 1990

Caron C, Rutter M: Comorbidity in child psychopathology: concepts, issues and research strategies. J Child Psychol Psychiatry 32:1063–1080, 1991

Cohen P, Cohen J, Kasen S, et al: An epidemiological study of disorders in late childhood and adolescence, I: age and gender-specific prevalence. J Child Psychol Psychiatry 34:851–867, 1993

Costello EJ: Child psychiatric epidemiology: implications for clinical research and practice, in Advances in Clinical Child Psychology, Vol 13. Edited by Lahey BB, Kazdin AE. New York, Plenum, 1990, pp 53–90

Costello EJ, Costello AJ, Edelbrock C, et al: Psychiatric disorders in pediatric primary care: prevalence and risk factors. Arch Gen Psychiatry 45:1107–1116, 1988

Edelbrock C, Costello AJ: Convergence between statistically derived behavior problem syndromes and child psychiatric disorders. J Abnorm Child Psychol 16:219–231, 1988

Esser G, Schmidt MH, Woerner W: Epidemiology and course of psychiatric disorders in school-age children: results of a longitudinal study. J Child Psychol Psychiatry 31:243–263, 1990

Feehan M, McGee R, Williams SM: Mental health disorders from age 15 to age 18 years. J Am Acad Child Adolesc Psychiatry 32:1118–1126, 1993

Fergusson DM, Horwood LJ, Lynskey MT: The effects of conduct disorder and attention deficit in middle childhood on offending and scholastic ability at age 13. J Child Psychol Psychiatry 34:899–916, 1993

Fleming JE, Offord DR, Boyle MH: Prevalence of childhood and adolescent depression in the community. Br J Psychiatry 155:647–654, 1989

Fleming JE, Boyle MH, Offord DR: The outcome of adolescent depression in the Ontario Child Health Study follow-up. J Am Acad Child Adolesc Psychiatry 32:28–33, 1993

Frost LA, Moffitt TE, McGee R: Neuropsychological correlates of psychopathology in an unselected cohort of young adolescents. J Abnorm Psychol 98: 307–313, 1989

Gould MS, Wunsch-Hitzig R, Dohrenwend B: Estimating the prevalence of childhood psychopathology. J Am Acad Child Adolesc Psychiatry 20:462–476, 1981

Gould MS, Bird H, Jaramillo BS: Correspondence between statistically derived behavior problem syndromes and child psychiatric diagnoses in a community sample. J Abnorm Child Psychol 21:287–313, 1993

Harrington R, Fudge H, Rutter M, et al: Adult outcomes of childhood and adolescent depression, II: links with antisocial disorders. J Am Acad Child Adolesc Psychiatry 30:434–439, 1991

Kashani JH, Beck NC, Hoeper EW, et al: Psychiatric disorders in a community sample of adolescents. Am J Psychiatry 144:584–589, 1987

Kashani JH, Orvaschel H, Rosenberg TK, et al: Psychopathology in a community sample of children and adolescents: a developmental perspective. J Am Acad Child Adolesc Psychiatry 28:701–706, 1989

Kendall PC, Clarkin JF: Introduction to special section: comorbidity and treatment implications. J Consult Clin Psychol 60:833–834, 1992

Kovacs M, Paulauskas S, Gatsonis C, et al: Depressive disorders in childhood, III: a longitudinal study of comorbidity with and (without) risk for conduct disorder. J Affect Disord 15:205–217, 1988

Kovacs M, Gatsonis C, Paulauskas S, et al: Depressive disorders in childhood, IV: a longitudinal study of comorbidity with and risk for anxiety disorders. Arch Gen Psychiatry 46:776–782, 1989

Lewinsohn PM, Rohde P, Seeley JR, et al: Comorbidity of unipolar depression, I: major depression with dysthymia. J Abnorm Psychol 100:205–213, 1991

Loeber R, Keenan K, Lahey GB, et al: Evidence for developmentally based diagnoses of oppositional defiant disorder and conduct disorder. J Abnorm Child Psychol 21:377–410, 1993

McGee R, Williams S: A longitudinal study of depression in nine-year-old children. J Am Acad Child Adolesc Psychiatry 27:342–348, 1988

McGee R, Williams S, Feehan M: Attention deficit disorder and age of onset of problem behaviors. J Abnorm Child Psychol 20:487–502, 1992a

McGee R, Feehan M, Williams S, et al: DSM-III disorders from age 11 to age 15 years. J Am Acad Child Adolesc Psychiatry 31:50–59, 1992b

Moffitt TE: Juvenile delinquency and attention deficit disorder: boys' developmental trajectories from age 3 to age 15. Child Dev 61:893–910, 1990

Offord DR, Boyle MH, Szatmari P, et al: Ontario Child Health Study, II: six-month prevalence of disorder and rates of service utilization. Arch Gen Psychiatry 44:832–836, 1987

Poznaski EO, Cook SC, Carroll BJ: A depression rating scale for children. Pediatrics 64:442–450, 1979

Rohde P, Lewinsohn PM, Seeley JR: Comorbidity of unipolar depression, II: comorbidity with other mental health disorders in adolescents and adults. J Abnorm Psychol 100:214–222, 1991

Rutter M: Isle of Wight revisited: twenty-five years of child psychiatric epidemiology. J Am Acad Child Adolesc Psychiatry 28:633–653, 1989

Spitzer RL, Endicott J: Education, Health, Behavior: Schedule for Affective Disorders and Schizophrenia—Lifetime Version. New York, Biometrics Research, 1975

Velez CN, Johnson J, Cohen P: A longitudinal analysis of selected risk factors for childhood psychopathology. J Am Acad Child Adolesc Psychiatry 28:861–864, 1989

Verhulst FC, Althaus M: Persistence and change in behavioral/emotional problems reported by parents of children aged 4–14: an epidemiological study. Acta Psychiatr Scand 77 (suppl 339):1–28, 1988

Verhulst GC, van der Ende J: "Comorbidity" in an epidemiological sample: a longitudinal perspective. J Child Psychol Psychiatry 34:767–783, 1993

12

Summary and Conclusions

Longitudinal studies are difficult to do well. Too short a study and the results may be meaningless. Too long a study and the subjects cannot be found, money runs out, and research methods become seriously out of date. Despite these problems, there have been some longitudinal studies done that have greatly advanced our understanding of the nature and treatment of psychopathology in childhood. Without these studies, much less would be known about the clinical course of important disorders, the effects of treatments, and the various risk and protective factors. None of these studies has been perfect. Some longitudinal studies did not focus on quite the right questions, some produced contradictory results, and others produced results that were hard to interpret.

What have we learned from the longitudinal studies reviewed in this Group for the Advancement of Psychiatry (GAP) report? Many of the things that we have learned have been surprising—even counterintuitive. Pre- and perinatal insults need not necessarily lead to serious consequences in later life. Premature infants, if raised in nondeprived settings, are not likely to be mentally retarded or learning disabled. Today, of course, premature infants who would not have been kept alive 15 years ago are surviving. Will this advancement lead to an untoward outcome? We do not know. New longitudinal studies need to be done.

Certain serious illnesses emerging later in childhood may be associated with a greater risk of psychopathology. This risk is true at least for those with asthma. Psychological factors, such as psychological stress, also may lead to exacerbation of asthmatic attacks. Whether other illnesses are associated with a greater risk of psychopathology simply has not been studied adequately.

Infant temperamental characteristics can be classified and measured; however, they appear to predict little in terms of later personality
development or psychopathology. Although temperamental characteristics measured in infancy correlate poorly with temperamental characteristics measured at age 4 or 5 years, they appear to be much more
stable and correlate well with temperament at ages 8 and 12 years. Some
of these temperamental characteristics, particularly aggressivity and
negativity at age 5 years, are serious risk factors for behavioral psychopathology at age 8 or 12 years and, possibly, at later ages as well. Aggressive, negative 5-year-olds do not necessarily grow out of their problems.
Their problems are important and should be dealt with when children
are age 5 years.

What does appear to be important is early language development.
Delays in language development or developmental language disorders
are risk factors for later psychopathology. Fifty percent of school-age
children with language problems requiring speech and language therapy also have diagnosable psychopathology.

Hyperactivity and short attention span are characteristics that tend
to persist into later childhood—even adulthood. Alone, each of these
characteristics may not be a risk factor for later psychopathology, but,
when accompanied by oppositional behavior and conduct disorder, the
outcome is detrimental to the child. Many studies have shown that children with these comorbid problems are at risk later for becoming delinquent and antisocial. Conduct disorder in childhood, which is much
more common in males, is a risk factor for later delinquency, even if it is
not associated with hyperactivity. Again, early intervention is important. The effects of comorbidity in this instance can be serious.
Comorbidity in general, especially as children grow older, leads to adverse social, academic, and psychopathological outcomes.

Depression does occur in children, in all of its adult manifestations.
Mania, in contrast, is rarely seen in children younger than age 12 years.
Depression in school-age children can be severe or mild. In contrast to
adolescents with depression, depressed children are more likely to have
somatic complaints and phobias rather than loss of interest in activities.
Depression in children, as in adults, may manifest itself episodically. A
child or an adolescent who has had one depressive episode is at high
risk for developing a second episode in the future, often within 2–5
years. In adolescents, the risk of suicide may be as great as in adults, and
a suicide attempt may be predictive of later successful suicide.

Depressed children are also more likely than nondepressed children to be anxious or to be diagnosed as having attention-deficit disorder with or without hyperactivity.

Anxiety disorder and obsessive-compulsive disorder are also seen in children. It is likely from what is known that obsessive-compulsive disorder in children is related to that seen in adults, but whether the anxiety disorders are so related remains to be seen. Other longitudinal studies are necessary.

Anorexia nervosa has a much more ominous prognosis than we thought in the past. Even those individuals who recover from their eating disorder later are liable to show other continuing psychopathology, including depression. As many as 50%–60% of adolescents with eating disorders continue to have the disorder at the end of 5 years, and some will die of it. Early onset, severe weight loss, and poor family relationships are all factors that predict poor outcome. Bulimia, often associated with anorexia, may have an equally negative outcome, but this is only inferred. Again, more longitudinal studies are required.

Childhood trauma, both acute and chronic, only recently has been investigated, which is surprising in view of the fact that it may have been around for many thousands of years. Even a single incident of severe trauma (such as the episode in Chowchilla in which 26 children were kidnapped by three men and held captive underground in a bus for 27 hours) will continue to exert its effects years later. Five years after the kidnapping episodes, the children had numerous fears, frightening dreams, and detailed (if at times erroneous) memories of the event. Their play was filled with reenactments of the trauma, and the children had a sense that there was no future for them. Meanwhile, the parents generally believed that their children had recovered fully from the trauma and suffered no ill effects. Some children who had witnessed a sniper attack at their school had symptoms of posttraumatic stress disorder (PTSD) 14 months later. Those who had received the greatest "dose" of exposure were the most likely to have PTSD.

Although the longitudinal studies discussed in this report reveal some important facts about psychopathology, they do not reveal what treatment works best. However, they do highlight some important observations about treatment. One of the most important factors to consider in planning treatment for a child is the functioning of his or her parents. Risk factors for the development of psychopathology in children are mental illness in the parents, such as severe depression or schizophrenia; parental alcohol or substance abuse; or parental violence. In certain instances, there may be an interaction between heredity and the relationship between parent and child. For example, a boy may inherit from his overly aggressive father a propensity toward aggression and then may be pushed by his abusive father to express his aggression to an even greater degree than he otherwise might have done. In other instances, it is likely that family chaos and violence are nonspecific risk factors that exacerbate psychopathology in family members. Mental health professionals who treat disturbed patients who are parents should always be concerned that their patients' children may be at risk for psychopathology and should inquire if the children may need evaluation and care.

A second lesson from longitudinal studies of treatment is that multidimensional treatment is better than a single modality treatment. Aggressive, hyperactive children who have conduct disorder may need medication, and their parents may need training in parental skills; the children themselves may benefit from psychotherapy, social skills training, and cognitive therapy. If children are seriously delinquent or out of control, temporary residential treatment may be needed as well. Longitudinal studies emphasize that the wise therapist must take into account multiple factors important to each child, including diagnosis; hereditary, temperamental, and personality factors; parental behavior and psychopathology; history of trauma and abuse; parents' need to learn new skills; responsiveness of the child to therapy; and efficacy of medication.

Beyond what we have learned about family factors associated with child and adolescent psychopathology, we also have learned that bold experiments initiated at the societal level, such as Project Head Start and the New Haven School Development Program, are effective in helping children and their families, although not always in ways that were initially anticipated. These programs should be expanded and strengthened, as indeed the United States government currently seems to be doing.

All of these findings summarize what the GAP Committee on Child Psychiatry has learned from its review of longitudinal studies of psychopathology in children and adolescents. As with most projects we undertake, we began with the expectation that committee members would learn from one another and from the literature we reviewed and discussed. It has been a profitable experience for us, and we hope that all practitioners find this report to be a useful one.

GAP Committees and Membership

Committee on Adolescence

Lois Flaherty, Bluebell, PA, *Chairperson*
Warren J. Gadpaille, Denver, CO
Robert Hendren, Piscataway, NJ
Harvey Horowitz, Philadelphia, PA
Silvio J. Onesti Jr., Belmont, MA

Committee on Aging

Gene D. Cohen, Washington, DC, *Chairperson*
Karen Blank, West Hartford, CT
Carl Cohen, Brooklyn, NY
Charles M. Gaitz, Houston, TX
Ira R. Katz, Philadelphia, PA
Andrew F. Leuchter, Los Angeles, CA
Gabe J. Maletta, Minneapolis, MN
Kenneth M. Sakauye, New Orleans, LA
Charles A. Shamoian, Larchmont, NY

Committee on Alcoholism and the Addictions

John A. Menninger, Denver, CO, *Chairperson*
Stephen Dilts, Denver, CO
Richard J. Frances, New Canaan, CT
William A. Frosch, New York, NY

Marc Galanter, New York, NY
Collins E. Lewis, St. Louis, MO
Earl A. Loomis Jr., Augusta, GA
Edgar P. Nace, Dallas, TX
Richard Suchinsky, Silver Spring, MD
John S. Tamerin, Greenwich, CT
Joseph Westermeyer, St. Paul, MN
Douglas Ziedonis, New Haven, CT

Committee on Child Psychiatry

Peter Jensen, Rockville, MD, *Co-Chairperson*
David A. Mrazek, Washington, DC, *Co-Chairperson*
William R. Beardslee, Woburn, MA
Penny Knapp, Sacramento, CA
John F. McDermott Jr., Honolulu, HI
Cynthia R. Pfeffer, White Plains, NY
John Schowalter, New Haven, CT
Theodore Shapiro, New York, NY
Peter E. Tanguay, Louisville, KY

Committee on College Students

Earle Silber, Chevy Chase, MD, *Chairperson*
Robert L. Arnstein, Hamden, CT
Varda Backus, La Jolla, CA
Harrison P. Eddy, White Plains, NY
Myron B. Liptzin, Chapel Hill, NC
Malkah Tolpin Notman, Brookline, MA
Peter Reich, Cambridge, MA
Elizabeth Aub Reid, Cambridge, MA
Lorraine D. Siggins, New Haven, CT
Morton Silverman, Chicago, IL
Tom G. Stauffer, White Plains, NY
Robert Wenger, Ambler, PA

Committee on Cultural Psychiatry

Ezra Griffith, New Haven, CT, *Chairperson*
Renato Alarcon, Decatur, GA
Irma Bland, New Orleans, LA

Edward F. Foulks, New Orleans, LA
Francis G. Lu, San Francisco, CA
Maria Oquendo, New York, NY
Pedro Ruiz, Houston, TX
Jose Arturo Silva, San Antonio, TX

Committee on Disabilities

Sanjay Gulati, Cambridge, MA, *Chairperson*
Meyer S. Gunther, Chicago, IL
Bryan King, Los Angeles, CA
Robert S. Nesheim, Duluth, MN
William H. Sack, Portland, OR
William A. Sonis, Philadelphia, PA
Margaret L. Stuber, Los Angeles, CA
Henry H. Work, Bethesda, MD

Committee on the Family

Frederick Gottlieb, Los Angeles, CA, *Chairperson*
W. Robert Beavers, Dallas, TX
Lee Combrinck-Graham, Stamford, CT
James Griffith, Vienna, VA
Henry U. Grunebaum, Cambridge, MA
Herta A. Guttman, Montreal, Canada
Lois Slovik, Boston, MA

Committee on Government Policy

Thomas L. Clannon, San Francisco, CA, *Chairperson*
Seymour Applebaum, Kew Gardens, NY
Edward Hanin, New York, NY
Naomi Heller, Washington, DC
Jeremy Lazarus, Denver, CO
Roger Peele, Washington, DC
John P. D. Shemo, Charlottesville, VA
William W. Van Stone, Washington, DC

Committee on Human Sexuality

Bertram H. Schaffner, New York, NY, *Chairperson*
Paul L. Adams, Louisville, KY

Jennifer Downey, New York, NY
Jack Drescher, New York, NY
Richard C. Friedman, New York, NY
Joan A. Lang, Galveston, TX
Joseph Merlino, New York, NY

Committee on International Relations

Vamik D. Volkan, Charlottesville, VA, *Chairperson*
Salman Akhtar, Philadelphia, PA
Letha B. Cole, Houston, TX
Robert M. Dorn, El Macero, CA
David R. Hawkins, Chapel Hill, NC
John S. Kafka, Washington, DC
Otto F. Kernberg, White Plains, NY
Rita R. Rogers, Palos Verdes Estates, CA
Stephen B. Shanfield, San Antonio, TX
Edward Shapiro, Stockbridge, MA

Committee on Medical Education

James Scully, Columbia, SC, *Chairperson*
Carol Bernstein, New York, NY
Leah J. Dickstein, Louisville, KY
Steven L. Dubovsky, Denver, CO
Saul I. Harrison, Torrance, CA
Harold I. Lief, Philadelphia, PA
Kathleen McKenna, Chicago, IL
Carol C. Nadelson, Boston, MA
Carolyn B. Robinowitz, Washington, DC
Stephen C. Scheiber, Deerfield, IL
Sidney L. Werkman, Washington, DC

Committee on Mental Health Services

W. Walter Menninger, Topeka, KS, *Chairperson*
Richard Bernstein, Burlington, VT
Mary Jane England, Roseland, NJ
Richard Lippincott, McMinnville, OR
Steven Mirin, Washington, DC
James Sabin, Boston, MA

Jose Maria Santiago, Tucson, AZ
Steven S. Sharfstein, Baltimore, MD
Altha J. Stewart, Philadelphia, PA
Michael J. Vergare, Philadelphia, PA
Jack A. Wolford, Pittsburgh, PA

Committee on Occupational Psychiatry

Robert Larsen, San Francisco, CA, *Chairperson*
Peter L. Brill, Radnor, PA
Duane Q. Hagen, St. Louis, MO
Barbara Long, Atlanta, GA
David E. Morrison, Palatine, IL
Clarence J. Rowe, St. Paul, MN

Committee on Planning and Communications

Paul J. Fink, Philadelphia, PA, *Chairperson*
Doyle I. Carson, Dallas, TX
Robert S. Garber, Longboat Key, FL
Robert W. Gibson, Towson, MD
Richard K. Goodstein, West Haven, CT
Richard Harding, Columbia, SC
Alan Newman, New Orleans, LA
Donald Ross, Towson, MD
Harvey L. Ruben, New Haven, CT
Melvin Sabshin, Washington, DC
Michael R. Zales, Tucson, AZ

Committee on Preventive Psychiatry

Brian J. McConville, Cincinnati, OH, *Chairperson*
Naomi Rae-Grant, London, Ontario, Canada
Hans Steiner, Palo Alto, CA
Warren T. Vaughan Jr., Woodside, CA

Committee on Psychiatry and the Community

Francine Cournos, New York, NY, *Co-Chairperson*
David Pollack, Portland, OR, *Co-Chairperson*
C. Knight Aldrich, Charlottesville, VA

Stephen Goldfinger, Boston, MA
David George Greenfield, Branford, CT
H. Richard Lamb, Los Angeles, CA
Kenneth Minkoff, Woburn, MA
John C. Nemiah, Hanover, NH
John J. Schwab, Louisville, KY
John A. Talbott, Baltimore, MD
Allan Tasman, Louisville, KY

Committee on Psychiatry and the Law

Joseph Satten, San Francisco, CA, *Chairperson*
Jeffrey S. Janofsky, Timonium, MD
Carl P. Malmquist, Minneapolis, MN
Jeffrey Metzner, Denver, CO
Betty J. Pfefferbaum, Oklahoma City, OK
Jonas R. Rappeport, Towson, MD
Phillip J. Resnick, Cleveland, OH
William D. Weitzel, Lexington, KY

Committee on Psychiatry and Religion

Richard C. Lewis, New Haven, CT, *Chairperson*
Naleen N. Andrade, Honolulu, HI
Keith G. Meador, Durham, NC
Abigail R. Ostow, Waban, MA
Sally K. Severino, Albuquerque, NM
Clyde R. Snyder, Chevy Chase, MD
Herzl R. Spiro, Milwaukee, WI

Committee on Psychopathology

Lisa Dixon, Baltimore, MD, *Chairperson*
David A. Adler, Boston, MA
Jeffrey Berlant, Boise, ID
Robert A. Dorwart, Cambridge, MA
Rebecca Dulit, White Plains, NY
James M. Ellison, Belmont, MA
Samuel G. Siris, Glen Oaks, NY

Committee on Public Education

Steven E. Katz, Portland, ME *Chairperson*
David Baron, Gwynedd Valley, PA

Jack W. Bonner III, Greenville, SC
Jeffrey L. Geller, Worcester, MA
Jeanne Leventhal, Hayward, CA
David Preven, Bronx, NY
Boris G. Rifkin, New Haven, CT
Andrew E. Slaby, New York, NY
Calvin R. Sumner, Buckhannon, WV
Laurence R. Tancredi, New York, NY

Committee on Research

Russell Gardner, Galveston, TX, *Chairperson*
Robert Cancro, New York, NY
John H. Greist, Madison, WI
Jerry M. Lewis, Dallas, TX
John G. Looney, Durham, NC
William Sledge, New Haven, CT
Zebulon Taintor, New York, NY

Committee on Social Issues

Martha J. Kirkpatrick, Los Angeles, CA, *Chairperson*
Ian E. Alger, New York, NY
Roderic Gorney, Los Angeles, CA
H. James Lurie, Seattle, WA
Theodore Nadelson, Jamaica Plain, MA
Perry Ottenberg, Philadelphia, PA
Jane L. Rosenthal, New York, NY
Miriam Rosenthal, Cleveland, OH

Committee on Therapeutic Care

Alan Gruenberg, Philadelphia, PA, *Chairperson*
Thomas E. Curtis, Chapel Hill, NC
Donald C. Fidler, Morgantown, WV
Donald W. Hammersley, Bethesda, MD
William B. Hunter III, Albuquerque, NM
Milton Kramer, Cincinnati, OH
John Lipkin, Perry Point, MA
Robert E. Switzer, Dunn Loring, VA

Committee on Therapy

Susan Lazar, Bethesda, MD, *Chairperson*
Gerald Adler, Boston, MA
Jules R. Bemporad, Mamaroneck, NY
Andrew P. Morrison, Cambridge, MA
William C. Offenkrantz, Carefree, AZ
Lawrence Rockland, White Plains, NY
Jay B. Rohrlich, New York, NY
Allan D. Rosenblatt, La Jolla, CA
Robert Waldinger, West Newton, MA

CONTRIBUTING MEMBERS

Kenneth Z. Altshuler, Dallas, TX
Spencer Bayles, Houston, TX
Elissa P. Benedek, Ann Arbor, MI
Renee L. Binder, San Francisco, CA
Mark Blotcky, Dallas, TX
H. Keith Brodie, Durham, NC
Robert N. Butler, New York, NY
Eugene M. Caffey Jr., Bowie, MD
Eric Caine, Rochester, NY
Robert J. Campbell, New York, NY
Ian Canino, New York, NY
J. Richard Ciccone, Rochester, NY
Park Dietz, Newport Beach, CA
James S. Eaton Jr., Washington, DC
Lloyd C. Elam, Nashville, TN
Joseph T. English, New York, NY
*Alexander Gralnick, Port Chester, NY
Joseph Green, Tucson, AZ
Barrie Greiff, Newton, MA
John Greist, Madison, WI
Johanna A. Hoffman, Scottsdale, AZ
Paulina Kernberg, White Plains, NY
Clarice Kestenbaum, New York, NY
Edward J. Khantzian, Haverhill, MA
Othilda M. Krug, Cincinnati, OH
Alan I. Levenson, Tucson, AZ

Norman L. Loux, Sellersville, PA
Alan A. McLean, Gig Harbor, WA
David Mendell, Houston, TX
Roy Menninger, Topeka, KS
Mary E. Mercer, Nyack, NY
Robert Michels, New York, NY
Andrew Morrison, Cambridge, MA
Joseph D. Noshpitz, Washington, DC
Herbert Pardes, New York, NY
Norman L. Paul, Lexington, MA
Harris Peck, New Rochelle, NY
Marvin E. Perkins, Roanoke, VA
George H. Pollock, Chicago, IL
Becky Potter, Tucson, AZ
Elise Richman, Scarsdale, NY
David Robbins, Chappagua, NY
David A. Soskis, Bala Cynwyd, PA
Jeffrey L. Speller, Cambridge, MA
Brandt F. Steele, Denver, CO
Terry Stein, East Lansing, MI
Bryce Templeton, Philadelphia, PA
Lenore Terr, San Francisco, CA
John A. Turner, San Francisco, CA
Paul Tyler Wilson, Bethesda, MD
Ronald Wintrob, Boston, MA
Howard Zonana, New Haven, CT

LIFE MEMBERS

C. Knight Aldrich, Charlottesville, VA
Robert L. Arnstein, Hamden, CT
Walter E. Barton, Hartland, VT
Viola W. Bernard, New York, NY
Henry W. Brosin, Tucson, AZ
John Donnelly, Hartford, CT
Merrill T. Eaton, Omaha, NE
O. Spurgeon English, Narberth, PA
Stephen Fleck, New Haven, CT
Jerome Frank, Baltimore, MD
Charles M. Gaitz, Houston, TX

Robert S. Garber, Longboat Key, FL
Robert I. Gibson, Towson, MD
Margaret M. Lawrence, Pomona, NY
Jerry M. Lewis, Dallas, TX
Harold I. Lief, Philadelphia, PA
Earl Loomis, Augusta, GA
Judd Marmor, Los Angeles, CA
Herbert C. Modlin, Topeka, KS
John C. Nemiah, Hanover, NH
William C. Offenkrantz, Scottsdale, AZ
Perry Ottenberg, Philadelphia, PA
Naomi Rae-Grant, London, Ontario, Canada
Melvin Sabshin, Washington, DC
Julius Schreiber, Washington, DC
Robert E. Switzer, Dunn Loring, VA
Warren T. Vaughan Jr., Woodside, CA
Jack A. Wolford, Pittsburgh, PA
Henry H. Work, Bethesda, MD
Michael R. Zales, Tucson, AZ

BOARD OF DIRECTORS

Officers

President
Malkah T. Notman
The Cambridge Hospital
54 Clark Road
Brookline, MA   02146

President-Elect
Stephen C. Scheiber
American Board of Psychiatry and Neurology
500 Lake Cook Road, Suite 335
Deerfield, IL   60015

Secretary
Joseph Westermeyer
1935 Summitt Avenue
St. Paul, MN   55105

Treasurer
Jack W. Bonner III
Behavioral Health Services
701 Grove Road
Greenville, SC   29605

Board Members
Carol Nadelson
Roger Peele
Harvey Ruben
Steven S. Sharfstein

Past Presidents

*William C. Menninger	1946–1951
Jack R. Ewalt	1951–1953
Walter E. Barton	1953–1955
*Sol W. Ginsburg	1955–1957
*Dana L. Farnsworth	1957–1959
*Marion E. Kenworthy	1959–1961
Henry W. Brosin	1961–1963
*Leo H. Bartemeier	1963–1965
Robert S. Garber	1965–1967
Herbert C. Modlin	1967–1969
John Donnelly	1969–1971
*George Tarjan	1971–1973
Judd Marmor	1973–1975
John C. Nemiah	1975–1977
Jack A. Wolford	1977–1979
Robert W. Gibson	1979–1981
*Jack Weinberg	1981–1982
Henry H. Work	1982–1985
Michael R. Zales	1985–1987
Jerry M. Lewis	1987–1989
Carolyn B. Robinowitz	1989–1991
*Allan Beigel	1991–1993
John Schowalter	1993–1995
Doyle I. Carson	1995–1997

PUBLICATIONS BOARD

David Adler, *Chairperson*
Robert L. Arnstein
James Ellison
Steve Katz
Joan Lang
John C. Nemiah
Jack McDermott

Consultants
C. Knight Aldrich
John C. Nemiah
Henry H. Work

CONTRIBUTORS

Bayer Corporation
Glaxo Wellcome, Inc.
Pharmacia & Upjohn, Inc.
Phillips Foundation
Wyeth-Ayerst Laboratories

GAP Publications

In the Long Run . . . Longitudinal Studies of Psychopathology in Children (GAP Report 143, 1998), Formulated by the Committee on Child Psychiatry

Addiction Treatment: Avoiding Pitfalls—A Case Approach (GAP Report 142, 1998), Formulated by the Committee on Alcoholism and Addictions

Alcoholism in the United States: Racial and Ethnic Considerations (GAP Report 141, 1996), Formulated by the Committee on Cultural Psychiatry

Adolescent Suicide (GAP Report 140, 1996), Formulated by the Committee on Adolescence

Mental Health in Remote Rural Developing Areas: Concepts and Cases (GAP Report 139, 1995), Formulated by the Committee on Therapeutic Care

Introduction to Occupational Psychiatry (GAP Report 138, 1994), Formulated by the Committee on Occupational Psychiatry

Forced Into Treatment: The Role of Coercion in Clinical Practice (GAP Report 137, 1994), Formulated by the Committee on Government Policy

Resident's Guide to Treatment of People With Chronic Mental Illness (GAP Report 136, 1993), Formulated by the Committee on Psychiatry and the Community

---

*Title is out of print.
†Available from Books on Demand, University Microfilms International, 300 North Zeeb Road, Ann Arbor, MI 48106-1346 (800-521-0600, ext. 3492).

Caring for People With Physical Impairment: The Journey Back (GAP Report 135, 1992), Formulated by the Committee on Handicaps

Beyond Symptom Suppression: Improving Long-Term Outcomes of Schizophrenia (GAP Report 134, 1992), Formulated by the Committee on Psychopathology

Psychotherapy in the Future (GAP Report 133, 1992), Formulated by the Committee on Therapy

Leaders and Followers: A Psychiatric Perspective on Religious Cults (GAP Report 132, 1992), Formulated by the Committee on Psychiatry and Religion

The Mental Health Professional and the Legal System (GAP Report 131, 1991), Formulated by the Committee on Psychiatry and the Law

*Psychotherapy With College Students (GAP Report 130, 1990), Formulated by the Committee on the College Student

A Casebook in Psychiatric Ethics (GAP Report 129, 1990), Formulated by the Committee on Medical Education

*Suicide and Ethnicity in the United States (GAP Report 128, 1989), Formulated by the Committee on Cultural Psychiatry

Psychiatric Prevention and the Family Life Cycle: Risk Reduction by Frontline Practitioners (GAP Report 127, 1989), Formulated by the Committee on Preventive Psychiatry

How Old Is Old Enough? The Ages of Rights and Responsibilities (GAP Report 126, 1989), Formulated by the Committee on Child Psychiatry

The Psychiatric Treatment of Alzheimer's Disease (GAP Report 125, 1988), Formulated by the Committee on Aging

Speaking Out for Psychiatry: A Handbook for Involvement With the Mass Media (GAP Report 124, 1987), Formulated by the Committee on Public Education

Us and Them: The Psychology of Ethnonationalism (GAP Report 123, 1987), Formulated by the Committee on International Relations

Psychiatry and Mental Health Professionals (GAP Report 122, 1987), Formulated by the Committee on Governmental Agencies

Interactive Fit: A Guide to Nonpsychotic Chronic Patients (GAP Report 121, 1987), Formulated by the Committee on Psychopathology

Teaching Psychotherapy in Contemporary Psychiatric Residency Training (GAP Report 120, 1986), Formulated by the Committee on Therapy

A Family Affair: Helping Families Cope With Mental Illness: A Guide for the Professions (GAP Report 119, 1986), Formulated by the Committee on Psychiatry and the Community

Crises of Adolescence—Teenage Pregnancy: Impact on Adolescent Development (GAP Report 118, 1986), Formulated by the Committee on Adolescence

The Family, the Patient, and the Psychiatric Hospital: Toward a New Model (GAP Report 117, 1985), Formulated by the Committee on Family

*Research and the Complex Causality of the Schizophrenias (GAP Report 116, 1984), Formulated by the Committee on Research

*Friends and Lovers in the College Years (GAP Report 115, 1983), Formulated by the Committee on the College Student

*Mental Health and Aging: Approaches to Curriculum Development (GAP Report 114, 1983), Formulated by the Committee on Aging

Community Psychiatry: A Reappraisal (GAP Report 113, 1983), Formulated by the Committee on Psychiatry and the Community

The Child and Television Drama (GAP Report 112, 1982), Formulated by the Committee on Social Issues

*The Process of Child Therapy (GAP Report 111, 1982), Formulated by the Committee on Child Psychiatry

The Positive Aspects of Long Term Hospitalization in the Public Sector for Chronic Psychiatric Patients (GAP Report 110, 1982), Formulated by the Committee on Psychopathology

Job Loss—A Psychiatric Perspective (GAP Report 109, 1982), Formulated by the Committee on Psychiatry in Industry

A Survival Manual for Medical Students (GAP Report 108, 1982), Formulated by the Committee on Medical Education

INTERFACES: A Communication Casebook for Mental Health Decision Makers (GAP Report 107, 1981), Formulated by the Committee on Mental Health Services

*Divorce, Child Custody and the Family (GAP Report 106, 1980), Formulated by the Committee on Family

*Mental Health and Primary Medical Care (GAP Report 105, 1980), Formulated by the Committee on Preventive Psychiatry

Psychiatric Consultation in Mental Retardation (GAP Report 104, 1979), Formulated by the Committee on Mental Retardation

*Self-Involvement in the Middle East Conflict (GAP Report 103, 1978), Formulated by the Committee on International Relations

The Chronic Mental Patient in the Community (GAP Report 102, 1978), Formulated by the Committee on Psychiatry and the Community

Power and Authority in Adolescence: The Origins and Resolutions of Intergenerational Conflict (GAP Report 101, 1978), Formulated by the Committee on Adolescence

*Psychotherapy and Its Financial Feasibility Within the National Health Care System (GAP Report 100, 1978), Formulated by the Committee on Therapy

*What Price Compensation? (GAP Report 99, 1977), Formulated by the Committee on Psychiatry in Industry

*Psychiatry and Sex Psychopath Legislation: The 30s to the 80s (GAP Report 98, 1977), Formulated by the Committee on Psychiatry and Law

Mysticism: Spiritual Quest or Psychic Disorder? (GAP Report 97, 1976), Formulated by the Committee on Psychiatry and Religion

*Recertification: A Look at the Issues (GAP Report 96, 1976), Formulated by the Ad hoc Committee on Recertification

*The Effect of the Method of Payment on Mental Health Care Practice (GAP Report 95, 1975), Formulated by the Committee on Governmental Agencies

*The Psychiatrist and Public Welfare Agencies (GAP Report 94, 1975), Formulated by the Committee on Psychiatry and the Community

*Pharmacotherapy and Psychotherapy: Paradoxes, Problems and Progress (GAP Report 93, 1975), Formulated by the Committee on Research

*The Educated Woman: Prospects and Problems (GAP Report 92, 1975), Formulated by the Committee on the College Student

*The Community Worker: A Response to Human Need (GAP Report 91, 1974), Formulated by the Committee on Therapeutic Care

*Problems of Psychiatric Leadership (GAP Report 90, 1974), Formulated by the Committee on Therapy

*Misuse of Psychiatry in the Criminal Courts: Competency to Stand Trial (GAP Report 89, 1974), Formulated by the Committee on Psychiatry and Law

Assessment of Sexual Function: A Guide to Interviewing (GAP Report 88, 1973), Formulated by the Committee on Medical Education

From Diagnosis to Treatment: An Approach to Treatment Planning for the Emotionally Disturbed Child (GAP Report 87, 1973), Formulated by the Committee on Child Psychiatry

*Humane Reproduction (GAP Report 86, 1973), Formulated by the Committee on Preventive Psychiatry

*The Welfare System and Mental Health (GAP Report 85, 1973), Formulated by the Committee on Psychiatry and Social Work

*The Joys and Sorrows of Parenthood (GAP Report 84, 1973), Formulated by the Committee on Public Education

*The VIP With Psychiatric Impairment (GAP Report 83, 1973), Formulated by the Committee on Governmental Agencies

*Crisis in Child Mental Health: A Critical Assessment (GAP Report 82, 1972), Formulated by the Ad hoc Committee

The Aged and Community Mental Health: A Guide to Program Development (GAP Report 81, 1971), Formulated by the Committee on Aging

*Drug Misuse: A Psychiatric View of a Modern Dilemma (GAP Report 80, 1970), Formulated by the Committee on Mental Health Services

*Toward a Public Policy on Mental Health Care of the Elderly (GAP Report 79, 1970), Formulated by the Committee on Aging

The Field of Family Therapy (GAP Report 78, 1970), Formulated by the Committee on Family

*Toward Therapeutic Care (2nd Edition—No. 51 revised) (GAP Report 77, 1970), Formulated by the Committee on Therapeutic Care

*The Case History Method in the Study of Family Process (GAP Report 76, 1970), Formulated by the Committee on Family

*The Right to Abortion: A Psychiatric View (GAP Report 75, 1969), Formulated by the Committee on Psychiatry and Law

*The Psychiatrist and Public Issues (GAP Report 74, 1969), Formulated by the Committee on International Relations

*Psychotherapy and the Dual Research Tradition (GAP Report 73, 1969), Formulated by the Committee on Therapy

*Crisis in Psychiatric Hospitalization (GAP Report 72, 1969), Formulated by the Committee on Therapeutic Care

*On Psychotherapy and Casework (GAP Report 71, 1969), Formulated by the Committee on Psychiatry and Social Work

*The Nonpsychotic Alcoholic Patient and the Mental Hospital (GAP Report 70, 1968), Formulated by the Committee on Mental Health Services

*The Dimensions of Community Psychiatry (GAP Report 69, 1968), Formulated by the Committee on Preventive Psychiatry

*Normal Adolescence (GAP Report 68, 1968), Formulated by the Committee on Adolescence

The Psychic Function of Religion in Mental Illness and Health (GAP Report 67, 1968), Formulated by the Committee on Psychiatry and Religion

*Mild Mental Retardation: A Growing Challenge to the Physician (GAP Report 66, 1967), Formulated by the Committee on Mental Retardation

*The Recruitment and Training of the Research Psychiatrist (GAP Report 65, 1967), Formulated by the Committee on Psychopathology

*Education for Community Psychiatry (GAP Report 64, 1967), Formulated by the Committee on Medical Education

*Psychiatric Research and the Assessment of Change (GAP Report 63, 1966), Formulated by the Committee on Research

*Psychopathological Disorders in Childhood: Theoretical Considerations and a Proposed Classification (GAP Report 62, 1966), Formulated by the Committee on Child Psychiatry

*Laws Governing Hospitalization of the Mentally Ill (GAP Report 61, 1966), Formulated by the Committee on Psychiatry and Law

*Sex and the College Student (GAP Report 60, 1965), Formulated by the Committee on the College Student

*Psychiatry and the Aged: An Introductory Approach (GAP Report 59, 1965), Formulated by the Committee on Aging

*Medical Practice and Psychiatry: The Impact of Changing Demands (GAP Report 58, 1964), Formulated by the Committee on Public Education

Psychiatric Aspects of the Prevention of Nuclear War (GAP Report 57, 1964), Formulated by the Committee on Social Issues

*Mental Retardation: A Family Crisis—The Therapeutic Role of the Physician (GAP Report 56, 1963), Formulated by the Committee on Mental Retardation

*Public Relations: A Responsibility of the Mental Hospital Administrator (GAP Report 55, 1963), Formulated by the Committee on Hospitals

*The Preclinical Teaching of Psychiatry (GAP Report 54, 1962), Formulated by the Committee on Medical Education

*Psychiatrists as Teachers in Schools of Social Work (GAP Report 53, 1962), Formulated by the Committee on Psychiatry and Social Work

The College Experience: A Focus for Psychiatric Research (GAP Report 52, 1962), Formulated by the Committee on the College Student

*Toward Therapeutic Care: A Guide for Those Who Work With the Mentally Ill (GAP Report 51, 1961), Formulated by the Committee on Therapeutic Care

*Problems of Estimating Changes in Frequency of Mental Disorders (GAP Report 50, 1961), Formulated by the Committee on Preventive Psychiatry

*Reports in Psychotherapy: Initial Interviews (GAP Report 49, 1961), Formulated by the Committee on Therapy

*Psychiatry and Religion: Some Steps Toward Mutual Understanding and Usefulness (GAP Report 48, 1960), Formulated by the Committee on Psychiatry and Religion

*Preventive Psychiatry in the Armed Forces: With Some Implications for Civilian Use (GAP Report 47, 1960), Formulated by the Committee on Governmental Agencies

*Administration of the Public Psychiatric Hospital (GAP Report 46, 1960), Formulated by the Committee on Hospitals

*Confidentiality and Privileged Communication in the Practice of Psychiatry (GAP Report 45, 1960), Formulated by the Committee on Psychiatry and Law

*The Psychiatrist and His Roles in a Mental Health Association (GAP Report 44, 1960), Formulated by the Committee on Public Education

*Basic Considerations in Mental Retardation: A Preliminary Report (GAP Report 43, 1959), Formulated by the Committee on Mental Retardation

*Some Observations on Controls in Psychiatric Research (GAP Report 42, 1959), Formulated by the Committee on Research

*Working Abroad: A Discussion of Psychological Attitudes and Adaptation in New Situations (GAP Report 41, 1958), Formulated by the Committee on International Relations

*Small Group Teaching in Psychiatry for Medical Students (GAP Report 40, 1958), Formulated by the Committee on Medical Education

*The Psychiatrist's Interest in Leisure-Time Activities (GAP Report 39, 1958), Formulated by the Committee on Public Education

The Diagnostic Process in Child Psychiatry (GAP Report 38, 1958), Formulated by the Committee on Child Psychiatry

*Emotional Aspects of School Desegregation (an abbreviated and less technical version of Report No. 37) (GAP Report 37A, 1960), Formulated by the Committee on Social Issues

*Psychiatric Aspects of School Desegregation (GAP Report 37, 1957), Formulated by the Committee on Social Issues

*The Person With Epilepsy at Work (GAP Report 36, 1957), Formulated by the Committee on Psychiatry in Industry

*The Psychiatrist in Mental Health Education: Suggestions on Collaboration With Teachers (GAP Report 35, 1956), Formulated by the Committee on Public Education

*The Consultant Psychiatrist in a Family Service Agency (GAP Report 34, 1956), Formulated by the Committee on Psychiatry and Social Work

*Therapeutic Use of the Self (A Concept for Teaching Patient Care) (GAP Report 33, 1955), Formulated by the Committee on Psychiatric Nursing

*Considerations on Personality Development in College Students (GAP Report 32, 1955), Formulated by the Committee on the College Student

*Trends and Issues in Psychiatric Residency Programs (GAP Report 31, 1955), Formulated by the Committee on Medical Education

*Report on Homosexuality With Particular Emphasis on This Problem in Governmental Agencies (GAP Report 30, 1955), Formulated by the Committee on Governmental Agencies

*The Psychiatrist in Mental Health Education (GAP Report 29, 1954), Formulated by the Committee on Public Education

*The Use of Psychiatrists in Government in Relation to International Problems (GAP Report 28, 1954), Formulated by the Committee on International Relations

*Integration and Conflict in Family Behavior (Reissued in 1968 as No. 27A) (GAP Report 27, 1954), Formulated by the Committee on Family

*Criminal Responsibility and Psychiatric Expert Testimony (GAP Report 26, 1954), Formulated by the Committee on Psychiatry and Law

*Collaborative Research in Psychopathology (GAP Report 25, 1954), Formulated by the Committee on Psychopathology

*Control and Treatment of Tuberculosis in Mental Hospitals (GAP Report 24, 1954), Formulated by the Committee on Hospitals

*Outline to Be Used as a Guide to the Evaluation of Treatment in a Public Psychiatric Hospital** (GAP Report 23, 1953), Formulated by the Committee on Hospitals

*The Psychiatric Nurse in the Mental Hospital** (GAP Report 22, 1952), Formulated by the Committee on Psychiatric Nursing—Committee on Hospitals

*The Contribution of Child Psychiatry to Pediatric Training and Practice** (GAP Report 21, 1952), Formulated by the Committee on Child Psychiatry

*The Application of Psychiatry to Industry** (GAP Report 20, 1951), Formulated by the Committee on Psychiatry in Industry

*Introduction to the Psychiatric Aspects of Civil Defense** (GAP Report 19, 1951), Formulated by the Committee on Governmental Agencies

*Promotion of Mental Health in the Primary and Secondary Schools: An Evaluation of Four Projects** (GAP Report 18, 1951), Formulated by the Committee on Preventive Psychiatry

*The Role of Psychiatrists in Colleges and Universities** (GAP Report 17, 1951), Formulated by the Committee on Academic Education

*Psychiatric Social Work in the Psychiatric Clinic** (GAP Report 16, 1950), Formulated by the Committee on Psychiatry and Social Work

*Revised Electro-Shock Therapy Report** (GAP Report 15, 1950), Formulated by the Committee on Therapy

*The Problem of the Aged Patient in the Public Psychiatric Hospital** (GAP Report 14, 1950), Formulated by the Committee on Hospitals

*The Social Responsibility of Psychiatry: A Statement of Orientation** (GAP Report 13, 1950), Formulated by the Committee on Social Issues

*Basic Concepts in Child Psychiatry** (GAP Report 12, 1950), Formulated by the Committee on Child Psychiatry

*The Position of Psychiatrists in the Field of International Relations** (GAP Report 11, 1950), Formulated by the Committee on International Relations

*Psychiatrically Deviated Sex Offenders** (GAP Report 10, 1950), Formulated by the Committee on Forensic Psychiatry

*The Relation of Clinical Psychology to Psychiatry** (GAP Report 9, 1949), Formulated by the Committee on Clinical Psychology

*An Outline for Evaluation of a Community Program in Mental Hygiene** (GAP Report 8, 1949), Formulated by the Committee on Cooperation With Lay Groups

*Statistics Pertinent to Psychiatry in the United States (GAP Report 7,
1949), Formulated by the Committee on Hospitals
*Research on Prefrontal Lobotomy (GAP Report 6, 1948), Formulated
by the Committee on Research
*Public Psychiatric Hospitals (GAP Report 5, 1948), Formulated by the
Committee on Hospitals
*Commitment Procedures (GAP Report 4, 1948), Formulated by the
Committee on Forensic Psychiatry
*Report on Medical Education (GAP Report 3, 1948), Formulated by the
Committee on Medical Education
*The Psychiatric Social Worker in the Psychiatric Hospital (GAP Re-
port 2, 1948), Formulated by the Committee on Psychiatric Social
Work
*Shock Therapy (GAP Report 1, 1947), Formulated by the Committee
on Therapy
Index to GAP Publications #1–#80

Symposia Reports

The Right to Die: Decision and Decision Makers (S-12, 1973), Formulated by the Committee on Aging
*Death and Dying: Attitudes of Patient and Doctor (S-11, 1965), For-
mulated by the Committee on Aging
*Urban America and the Planning of Mental Health Services (S-10,
1964), Formulated by the Committee on Preventive Psychiatry
*Pavlovian Conditioning and American Psychiatry (S-9, 1964), Formu-
lated by the Committee on Research
*Medical Uses of Hypnosis (S-8, 1962), Formulated by the Committee
on Medical Education
*Application of Psychiatric Insights to Cross-Cultural Communica-
tion (S-7, 1961), Formulated by the Committee on International Re-
lations
*The Psychological and Medical Aspects of the Use of Nuclear Energy
(S-6, 1960), Formulated by the Committee on Social Issues
*Some Considerations of Early Attempts in Cooperation Between Re-
ligion and Psychiatry (S-5, 1958), Formulated by the Committee on
Psychiatry and Religion

*Methods of Forceful Indoctrination: Observations and Interviews (S-4, 1957), Formulated by the Committee on Social Issues
*Factors Used to Increase the Susceptibility of Individuals to Forceful Indoctrination: Observations and Experiments (S-3, 1956), Formulated by the Committee on Social Issues
*Illustrative Strategies for Research in Psychopathology in Mental Health (S-2, 1956), Formulated by the Committee on Psychopathology
*Considerations Regarding the Loyalty Oath as a Manifestation of Current Social Tension and Anxiety (S-1, 1954), Formulated by the Committee on Social Issues

Films

*Discussion Guide to the Film (2, 1970)
*A Nice Kid Like You (1, 1970)

Index

*Page numbers printed in **boldface** type refer to tables or figures.*